GERMAN WARTIME M

Two-Wheeled
Blitzkrieg

GERMAN WARTIME MOTORCYCLES

Two-Wheeled Blitzkrieg

PAUL GARSON

AMBERLEY

Autobahn Escort
A solo rider leads a convoy of vehicles along the autobahn road network. Its construction started before Hitler came to power and was then enlarged by the Nazi state as a means for allowing the efficient movement of heavy motorized vehicles, especially tanks. In the last days of the war sections also served as emergency aircraft runways.

First published 2017

Amberley Publishing
The Hill, Stroud
Gloucestershire, GL5 4EP

www.amberley-books.com

Copyright © Paul Garson 2017

The right of Paul Garson to be identified as the Author
of this work has been asserted in accordance with the
Copyrights, Designs and Patents Act 1988.

British Library Cataloguing in Publication Data.
A catalogue record for this book is available from the British Library.

ISBN 978 1 4456 7236 6 (print)
ISBN 978 1 4456 7237 3 (ebook)

Origination by Amberley Publishing.
Printed in Great Britain.

Contents

Preface

This book was conceived as a visual history based on rare, original photographs, documents and illustrations and focusing on the motorcycle as an implement of war – in particular as a strategic adjunct of Germany's military juggernaut that ravaged the European continent during two world wars. Rather than a technical perspective, the emphasis focuses on the 'personal' elements of riders and their machines as well as the historical context in which they took part. All photos are reproduced from originals contained in the author's archives and were for the most part taken by ordinary German soldiers with their personal cameras. The photographs were collected over a twelve-year period from several European countries as well as sources in the US, Canada, South America and the Middle East.

Cameras at War
By the 1930s cameras and photography had reached an advanced evolutionary state, with Germany at the frontline in camera technology with brands such as Agfa, Contax, Exakta, Ihagee, Korelle, Leica, Rolleiflex, Voigtländer and Zeiss Ikon. These included the new 35 mm format and colour film.

Transporting War
German troops rumble, ride, cycle, trudge and tread along a dusty road in the French countryside during the summer 1940 invasion. In the foreground a bicycle trooper leads the way, followed by heavy draught horses pulling a pneumatic wheeled wagon, with a lone motorcyclist joining the cavalcade. Lying derelict at the side of the road are French tanks and military cars while in the far distance more German cyclists and infantry foot soldiers advance.

Introduction

Motorcycles have been going to war as long as there have motorcycles around to go to war. They were recruited for the battlefield thanks to their merits of speed, maneuverability and adaptability as a weapons platform – not to mention their cost effectiveness when compared to other mechanized implements of modern warfare.

By the beginning of the twentieth century, motorcycle production was a worldwide phenomenon, establishing iconic marques including the American Harley-Davidson and Indian; British Triumph, BSA Matchless and Norton; Italian Moto Guzzi and Gilera; French Terot, Rene Gillet and Gnome-Rhône; Belgian FN; and the German BMW, NSU, DKW, and Zündapp. The demands of the battlefront would spur further innovation and advancement.

Motorcycles were first introduced into the German military arsenal in 1904 when fourteen NSU machines appeared during the Imperial Maneuvers. By 1911, with the addition of sidecars that could carry additional men, weapons and material, some 5,400 machines joined the German army during the First World War of 1914–18. These were mostly machines built by NSU for army use while the Wanderer served as standard issue for the fledgling German air force. By the 1920s new terms entered the common vernacular: 'rad' and 'krad', the shortened form of the words *motorad* and *kraftrad*, German for motorcycle.

A count of late 1920s German motorcycle manufacturers indicates that over 500 different brands were in existence. However, the post-First World War German economy was in a state of collapse from hyperinflation with right-wing and left-wing factions battling in the streets – the fertile ground in which National Socialism sank its dark roots, but also the setting in which motorcycle sales were experiencing a major slump. That ended in 1933, not coincidentally as the Nazi party took control of the country with Adolf Hitler appointed as Chancellor. In that year German citizens were exempted from paying taxes on motorcycles, with German sales also being encouraged due to a limit placed on imported machines. Sales were further fuelled in 1935 by the purchase by the Wehrmacht of large numbers of machines for use by their motorcycle rifle troops.

As Nazi Germany militarized the entire country's industrial and social structure, placing it on a war footing, some 20,000,000 Germans donned uniforms. Some flew in the Luftwaffe or sailed in the Kriegsmarine. Many others slogged on foot in the Heer (regular Army) with some wearing the Totenkopf 'death's head' insignia of the SS and Waffen-SS. In addition, tens of thousands rode to war on motorcycles and were destined to play an important role across a wide variety of terrains and weather conditions, during which they served as couriers and scouts as well as highly mobile rifle and assault troops.

Of all the Second World War combatant nations, the German military was the largest employer of motorcycles and, in addition to those produced in Germany and Austria, the Wehrmacht acquired a variety of Belgian, British, Czech, and French machines as the Third Reich swept across conquered lands.

The new mechanized lightning war, or blitzkrieg, required motorcycles of high calibre in more ways than one. Although horses and even bicycles carried battalions of combatants, as did trucks and tracked vehicles, motorcycles often led the way. Purpose-built military machines as well as requisitioned civilian models were often transported along with their owners from civilian streets to the battlefield.

What did the German soldier think of their iron warhorses? The following was reported by German military historian Horst Hinrichsen, the words of a German soldier appearing in a letter written to the NSU factory:

On 21 September, it has been five years since I bought it new at your Stuttgart branch, where I worked as a mechanic since August 1939. Since the end of August I have been in Wehrmacht service with the motorcycle, which I myself have always driven since then. During the four years of my private driving, the machine always functioned to my complete satisfaction, as it has now, since I have been drafted. In this year I have driven it 20,000 km, at first in the Polish campaign, then during service in the operational area of the western front and on duty in France. During the campaign in France I drove about 7,000 km... If possible, I want to buy back the machine after the end of the war we have been compelled to wage.

The letter was penned in the early part of the war when Germany seemed invincible. There is no word if the satisfied customer was ever able to claim his beloved motorcycle.

The German army recognised the special role played by the motorcyclist, who was often a single man operating without support or cover against great odds, and responsible for delivering vital information. In 1942 the Motor Service Vehicle Medal was created, with motorcycle riders being eligible after ninety days of action (other vehicles required 185). To earn the medal, an individual rider was required to 'drive while under enemy contact; particularly involving great daily accomplishment in terms of distance, or particularly difficult road conditions, or driving under unusually harsh weather conditions'. The conditions included oceans of mud in Russia and endless tracks of windswept African sands, yet those requirements were met. However, once the medal was earned it could be withdrawn if the recipient caused an accident or damaged his bike through careless maintenance. A rider could survive the hellish warfare on the Eastern Front, then lose his medal of honour for breaking the speed limit.

On 22 June 1941, Germany launched Operation Barbarossa – the 3 million-man invasion of the Soviet Union. During the campaigns that followed, motorcycles served a wide variety of battlefield functions as well as providing a chauffeur service for officers, transporting the wounded and delivering hot meals to frontline troops. As with all motorcyclists, there was a kinship among these soldiers, who called themselves *kradmelder*. They rode exposed without the armour plating of the panzers, and without the shielding support of grenadier foot soldiers marching beside them. While confronting mine fields, artillery fire, and strafing aircraft, in effect they were moving targets and 'sniper magnets'.

Their other enemy was the Russian weather. By the first autumn of the invasion the roads had been transformed by the rains into nearly impassable bogs and the fields over which the motorcycles travelled were now 'seas of jelly three feet or more deep' where pack horses sank to their bellies and boots were sucked off the soldiers' feet.

Special Kit Reserved for the Motorcycle Trooper
Standing before a DKW NZ350, both *kradschützen* wear the much-prized *kradmantel* – the M1934 vulcanised motorcycle overcoat. This special all-weather coat was sought after by other soldiers and civilians alike. The rubberized watertight material afforded the motorcyclist much-needed protection against the elements. Air circulated through a design of inner panels for cooling in the summer heat and buttons allowed it to be snapped around the legs to block the winter cold. Other official gear included goggles, a knitted pullover and gloves.

Motorized forces that had once travelled over seventy miles in a day now were lucky to make ten. By winter, temperatures plummeted to -40 degrees; engine oil and exposed soldiers froze solid, with 113,000 cases of frostbite reported. A relatively few German motorcycle riders benefited from special heating systems later grafted onto their bikes, including foot and hand warmers.

In an effort to improve the design of their motorcycles, BMW sent designers to the front lines. One such specialist sent to the Russian Front reported the following:

> While we were following the movement of the front in daily stages, we spent the nights in tents on the steppes… We had crossed the Don, and then gone in the direction of Stalingrad, and we sought out the field repair shops which operated in the most primitive conditions directly behind the front line. There the machines were examined and reports on the troops' experiences were taken. My opinion was correct. The machines went under the liquid mud which flowed over the motors by the bucketful and was sucked into the low-lying air filter, ruining it. The mud got into the motor and often the oil pans no longer held oil, but only sand… One clearly saw the enormous difference between the soldiers out there on the Front and the back-line people, who were real bureaucrats while the troops were trying to build one usable machine out of ten ruined ones. The new oil filter on my machine, screwed onto the tank high up, performed without trouble. But the improvements – although we worked on them day and night to change the whole series at once – were no longer sufficient for Russia. Stalingrad had changed everything. All the machines that went to the East were lost, at least we never heard of them again.

By war's end, few of the motorcycles, along with their riders, ever returned home. Of the 20 million Germans who went to war in one form or another, 10 million were casualties, dead, wounded or captured. The Russians alone lost 30 million or more killed. For many of those lost in the all-consuming war of attrition, only the photographs remain.

The Machines Go To War

Specifications given for maximum speed and range vary depending on actual carrying load and terrain. The suffixes 'W' and 'WH' referred to special Wehrmacht production.

By 1938 some 200,000 motorcycles were produced in Germany and the adjacent areas annexed by Greater Germany or the Reich. The principal bikes included BMW, DKW, NSU, Triumph (under German license), Victoria and Zündapp. For heavy-duty sidecar use, the German military relied upon the Zündapp KS750 and the BMW R75, with both companies also making their own sidecars although those built by Stoye, Royal and Steib were also employed. Next in line were the lighter weight motorcycles manufactured by DKW and NSU. Non-German motorcycles, bought under license, included Triumph, with more than 12,000 250cc units built in Nuremberg, which was also home to Steib sidecars at the time.

Multi-Tasking for War
German newspaper and magazine advertisements reminded the public that the BMW company produced aircraft engines, motorcycles and trucks for the Wehrmacht. This example appeared in the March 20 1943 German motorcycle specialty publication *Das Motorrad*. A few weeks earlier, on 2 February, the German 6th Army survivors had surrendered to Soviet forces at the battle of Stalingrad, signalling the beginning of the end of the Third Reich.

Major Motorcycle Manufacturers Enlisted by the Wehrmacht

BMW Motorrad

While the company produced aircraft engines during the First World War, the 496cc R32, launched in 1923, was the first motorcycle badged under the BMW (Bayeriche Motoren Werke – Bavarian Motor Works) name. Its iconic 'boxer' twin-cylinder, air-cooled engine design quickly established a reputation for dependability, comfort and performance, which was further enhanced when it broke the motorcycle speed record using a special aerodynamically designed supercharged 750cc machine in 1937, reaching 173.68 mph. Then, in June 1939, three months prior to the start of the Second World War, German rider George Meier took top honours at the famous Isle of Man TT – the first for a foreign rider on a foreign (that is non-British) motorcycle. In addition to the vaunted 750cc R75, BMW also supplied the military with more than 36,000 sidevalve R12 BMWs. All told, the Wehrmacht utilized the following models: R4, R12, R23, R35 and R75.

BMW R4 (1932–37)

The BMW R4 was a 12 hp single-cylinder, four-stroke of 398cc displacement, mounted in a sturdy pressed steel frame and was, like all BMWs, shaft-driven via its enclosed driveshaft, doing away with the complications and maintenance of an exposed chain drive. The air-cooled, three-speed transmission machine required kick-starting. The solo mount machine featured a tell-tale curved girder front end. Tipping the scales at 414.4 lb, it could reach 62 mph (100 kmh) with a range of 211 miles (340 km). Some 15,000 were built. It was well received by both police and army operators.

BMW R12 (1935–42)

The R12 was powered by a 745cc four-stroke sidevalve engine, housed within a pressed steel frame, which produced 18 hp. The machine weighing some 414 lb, and in military spec could attain speeds of 62 mph with a range of 174 miles. Some 36,000 were built for the German military – more than any other motorbike in the BMW range. It would be replaced by more robust R75 sidecar combination.

BMW R23 (1938–49)
A 247cc single-cylinder four-stroke producing 10 hp. Some 8,000 of this lightweight machine were built.

BMW R35 (1937–40)
A single-cylinder 340cc four-stroke, making 14 hp, it had the same weight, maximum speed and range of the R4, which it replaced. Some 15,386 were built pre-war, with many civilian-owned models also requisitioned for military use. Weighing some 360 lb in military trim, it was capable of a top speed of 60 mph.

BMW R75 (solo) (1941–44)
Powered by a 746cc flathead with an overhead valve twin-cylinder four-stroke engine producing 26 hp, it could reach speeds of 57 mph with a range of 211 miles. It was first produced in 1938 as the result of Wehrmacht requests and saw service both in Europe and North Africa.

BMW R-75 Sidecar (1941–44)
Also known as the 'Type Russia,' the motorcycle/sidecar outfit (*kraftrad mit beiwagen*) was highly manoeuvrable and literally unstoppable until it encountered the Russian rainy season's mud and the snow drifts outside Stalingrad. Designed during 1939–41, the tank-tough R75, combined with its crankshaft-driven, third-wheel sidecar, proved itself a major success, clocking 52 miles to the US gallon with a range of 225 miles. It could climb 40-degree inclines as well as provide a carrying capacity of over 1,000 lb, which was about equal to its own 929-lb weight. Specifications included a 745cc air-cooled, four-stroke OHV twin cylinder engine that produced 26 hp at 4000 rpm. An eight-speed transmission included two reverse gears while a top speed was a reported 60 mph. However, it arrived too late in the war and in too small numbers (16,510) to affect the final outcome as its factory in Eisenach was destroyed in 1944 by Allied bombing. Today it is a most sought after collectible, fetching as much as $45,000 or more.

DKW

Established in Zschopau, located in the Ore Mountains some 14 km south-east of the Saxon city of Chemnitz, the Dampf-Kraft-Wagen company was founded in 1919 by a Danish entrepreneur, J. S. Rasmussen. It became the largest brand not only in the German Reich, but at one point in the world. By 1928 DKW was producing some 65,000 engines annually, powering some sixty different German inter-war motorcycle brands. Success came with the development of an innovative engine design based on the Schnuerle two-stroke loop scavenging process that eliminated the need of a deflector piston and improved the combustion process, which was further enhanced by improved exhaust ports. DKW applied all of this to their highly successful commercially produced RT 125, with 'RT' standing for 'Reichstyp' or National Model. In 1932 the company merged with Auto Union – composed of car makers DKW, Audi, Horch and Wanderer. German military motorcycle models included the RT125 and NZ350. Post-war, the proliferation of RT designs led to the development of several other motorcycle company models including the now iconic BSA Bantam and the Harley-Davidson Hummer as well as the Yamaha YA-1.

DKW RT 125 (1939–41), RT 125-1 (1943–45)

With a dry weight of 200.6 lb, the 123cc single-cylinder two-stroke, producing a mere 4.75 hp, could reach 44.7 mph with a range of 223 miles. A combined total of 33,000 units were built.

DKW NZ 350 (1934–38), NZ 350-1 (1944–45)

As the war raged in the East, the Wehrmacht was in need of an 'updated' machine for Army service so in 1943, DKW, having first developed the design in 1939 as a civilian model, brought out the new NZ 350. The military version required few changes, including a different front fender, thus dispensing with the original art deco look in favour of a slimmer, more functional and lighter design to reduce the jamming effects of battlefield mud. It was painted *schwarz-grau* (black-grey) for the Luftwaffe and *dunkel-grau* (or 'Sahara' beige) for Army use.

Although the focus of repeated Allied bombing raids, the Zschopau factory managed to continue production of the Wehrmacht issue NZ350. Powered by a 346cc single-cylinder two-stroke, it produced 11.5 hp at 4,000 rpm. The last years of the war saw shrinking production of the heavy-duty and more expensive Zündapp sidecar outfits. However, a combined total of some 57,000 were built, making it the most prolific of all German wartime motorcycles.

But it was the DKW 125 and 350 that served as the staple of the Wehrmacht's motorcycle corps. At war's end, the DKW factory, now in Soviet-controlled territory, was transformed into the MZ brand as produced by East Germany.

NSU

The marque's name was derived from the Neckar and the Sulm rivers that surrounded the city of its manufacture, Neckarsulm, and thus the letters NSU were adopted in 1892. The company, formed in 1873 by mechanics Heinrich Stoll and Christian Schmidt, first produced knitting machines in the early industrial age, then moved on to bicycles and automobiles. During the First World War NSU built both cars and motorcycles for the military, and also shared development of the prototype 'Beetle' for Ferdinand Porsche that eventually appeared as the Volkswagen – Hitler's 'people's car'. NSU motorcycle models, all single-cylinder, included the Pony 100, 201 ZDB, 251 OSL, 351 OSL, 601 OSL, 501 TS and 601 TS and, specifically for Wehrmacht use, the 251 OS and the unusual Opel-engined half-tracked Kettenkrad NSU HK10. NSU also built the 501 OSL in solo and sidecar versions (1935–39) as used by the Wehrmacht. Shortly before the war ended, the Neckarsulm factory was damaged by Allied bombing. NSU would eventually be acquired by Volkswagen in 1969.

NSU 251 OSL/OSL-WH (1933–1943)
Of four-stroke design, the 241cc single-cylinder machine, producing 9, 10 or 10.5 hp, reached 57 mph with a range of 217 miles. Mass production saw 35,000 in operation.

NSU 500 OSL
Produced from 1935 to 1939, the 494cc overhead cam single-cylinder engine produced 22 hp and offered a top speed of 80 mph. The sport machine gained a reputation as one of the fastest German machines of its day and also as very reliable. Relatively lavish in appointments, it also featured a twist grip throttle and could be fitted with a set of high exhaust pipes.

NSU Sd.Flz.2 Kettenkrad
The tracked Kettenkrad, powered by a four-cylinder, water-cooled Opel OHV engine, came in two variations, first as a troop carrier and tractor/tow vehicle and secondly as the specialised Kleine Kettenkrad fur Feldfernkabel Sd.Kfz. 2/1 variant, which carried and dispensed large spools of heavy communications field cable. As a tow vehicle it could haul a small cargo-carrying trailer or pull a 20 mm anti-aircraft gun or a 37 mm anti-tank cannon. It could carry 2,726 lb including the driver while in combat, with the weight including a crew of three totalling some 3,444 lb. The official manual listed a top speed of 44 mph while other sources claimed 38 and 50 mph. As well as scaling ravines and traversing ditches, it could ford streams 18 inches deep.

Puch
The Austrian company of Puch, based in Graz and founded by Johann Puch in 1899, began, as did many companies, with bicycles, ramping up to motorcycles in 1906, then automobiles in 1914. Puch gained fame in 1931 when it won the German Grand Prix. During its Third Reich era, after its assimilation in 1934 as a subsidiary of the Steyr-Daimler-Puch conglomerate, it grew into one of Europe's largest manufacturers. Eventually repurposed for war production, it benefited, as did some forty other German companies, from the use of slave labour drawn from the notorious Mauthausen-Gusen concentration camp system. Among its civilian models requisitioned for Wehrmacht service was the Puch S4, which was often employed by courier riders. Production of motorcycles and cars resumed after the war.

Victoria
Victoria started out as a bicycle maker in 1886, introducing its first motorcycle in 1899. The Nuremberg facility later added an engine factory in Munich, the power plant being designed by an ex-BMW engineer. In 1926 their supercharged racer broke the speed record with 104 mph. In the 1930s they began producing two- and four-stroke machines from 98cc to 248cc displacement. German military units included the KR 35 W and K 6.

Victoria KR 35 W (1938–45)
Powered by a 342cc four-stroke, single cylinder engine producing 18 hp and weighing
341.7 lb dry, it could reach 62 mph with a range of 248 miles.

Zündapp
Established in 1917 and located in Nuremberg, the company's name was formed by the
merger of two companies, Friedrich Krupp and the machine tool manufacturer Thiel,
under the name Zünder-un Apparatebau, translated from the German as 'Igniter and
Apparatus'. Zündapp then began building high-quality motorcycles in both two- and
four-stroke engine designs. By 1933 the company had produced 100,000 motorcycles.
The best known Zündapp was the KS 750 flat twin built exclusively for the German
army. Other military models included the DB 200, K 500 W, KS 600 W, K 800 W, and
KS 750.

Zündapp KS600KSW
During 1938–41 some 18,000 machines were produced. It differed from its KS 500
predecessor in having an enlarged engine displacement as well as a larger fuel tank and
an optional hand-operated gear change lever mounted on the right side of the upper
frame member. The twin-cylinder engine, bolted into a pressed steel frame, produced
28 hp working through a four-speed gearbox and BMW-like enclosed shaft-drive.
Steering was directed through a girder-type front fork. The bike in solo form weighed
205 kg (450 lb) and in sidecar form 507 kg (1,100 lb) with a maximum speed of 120
km/h solo and 100 km/h with sidecar, often a Steib BW 38 supplied exclusively to the
Wehrmacht. The 600 model was ultimately replaced by the KS 750.

Zündapp KS750 Sidecar Combination
Housed in a pressed steel frame, the transverse 751cc twin-cylinder made 26 hp and
featured eight gears, divided into four forward and four reverse and integrated along
with the power-driven sidecar. The KS 750 went into production in 1940, with an
estimated 18,695 units built. Weight was 920 lb with a top speed of 60 mph. It was
frequently equipped with the lethal M34, later the M43, light machine gun attached to
the sidecar. It was eventually seen as superior to the BMW R75 sidecar also in military
service. Then in 1942, a Zündapp-BMW hybrid was designed, the BW 43, which
saw a driven BMW 286/1 sidecar grafted onto a Zündapp KS 750. In addition, both
companies agreed to standardise some 70 per cent of both machines' components, thus
simplifying production and repairs.

Zündapp K800
The evolutionary design featured a flat-four engine and shaft drive, and was the only
four-cylinder powered machine employed by the Wehrmacht during the war. Its engine
design would later be employed by Japan's Honda to create the iconic Goldwing
motorcycle line.

The Clone Wars

Soviet dictator Joseph Stalin himself established the IMZ-Ural motorcycle brand in 1941, specifically to build copies of the BMW R75 as combat vehicles for the Red Army. Ultimately, 10,000 of these went to war. They were built in Siberia in a factory east of the Urals, thus their name, which is still home to the modern Ural. It went into production in the mid-1950s as the civilian M-72. Then in 1993 the 1940s BMW clone was updated both mechanically and cosmetically. At last estimate there are more than 3,000,000 on and off the road, mostly in Eastern Europe and Russia. The Chinese Communists, also acquiring Russian copies of German Second World War BMWs, came up with their own variations, including the Yangtze 750 and Changjiang as employed by the Chinese Army.

During the Second World War, the American Harley-Davidson company, in response to requests from the US military for a machine following the performance parameters of the German BMW K75, designed the Model XA. Also shaft-driven, it was a virtual copy of the original but was powered by a sidevalve twin-cylinder engine based on the German R71 – the predecessor to the R75. Producing 23 hp and capable of 63 mph, some 1,000 were built during 1942–43 but it was eclipsed by the advent of the all-purpose, four-wheel drive Jeep.

Transition/Experiment – Honing the Tools of Mechanized Warfare

1889 – British Leap Forward
The 1889 'Motor Scout' was powered by a 238cc single-cylinder engine and was armed with a Maxim machine gun, the contrivance carrying 1,000 rounds of ammunition and 120 miles of fuel capacity. It was designed and built by British manufacturer Frederick Reginald Simms, whose vision of future wars saw new-fangled motor-cars and machine guns merging together on the battlefield. Tanks, however, won the day as they offered a bit more protection.

Coming and Going – 'Latest Invention in War Machines'
An early 1900s design by the E. J. Pennington company of Coventry, the 'Military Autocar' carried two 'rapid firing guns' and four soldiers with 10,000 rounds of ammunition. Powered by a 16 hp engine capable of 45 mph, it rolled on four-inch-wide solid rubber tires. Fitted with 'regulation bullet proof' armour, the forward and rear-facing guns could be adjusted to fire between 50 and 700 rounds per minute. It did not see widespread production.

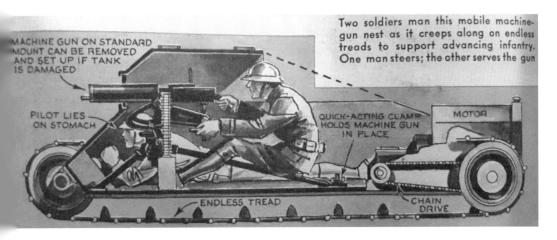

Pre-war Yankee Design
This illustration for a two-man 'mobile machine-gun nest' appeared in a popular US science magazine focusing on the miniaturization of military weapons for the envisioned new warfare. While armed with a tank-tough water-cooled Browning machine gun, the concept was never put into battlefield action.

Belated French Prototype

Dated to 1939, the LeHaitre Tractor Cycle, with its single tank tread design, was purportedly capable of 25 mph. Also intended for the new 'modern' war, it arrived belatedly, but the six-week war in the summer of 1940 prevented any further development or manufacture.

Opposite above: French Mobile AA12

The Rene Gillet sidevalve twin, first introduced in 1920, was available in both the G model (750cc) and the J model (1,000cc displacement). The rugged machines were compared favourably with Harley-Davidsons of the time and were popular with French police and military before the Second World War. Producing 14 hp, it could reach 67 mph, its clutch being operable by either foot or hand. It was strong enough to combine with a sidecar and its quick-detach wheel for ease of maintenance added to its popularity with the military. This example has been fitted with a Hotchkiss MLE 1914 light machine gun – a standard of the French army. The intent was to create a mobile anti-aircraft weapon, which is perhaps emphasized by the operator dressed in flight gear. Note the weapon's case attached to the motorcycle's frame.

Opposite below: German Motorcycle Tank and Iconic Insignia

German First World War designers experimented with a variety of confabulations while seeking 'modern' weapons that could negotiate the quagmire of trench warfare. This one-man treaded tank bristled with machine guns as well as a forward-mounted small-calibre cannon. Maintaining an upright position may have posed a problem since righting the vehicle once it had toppled on its side may have required more than the single occupant could have managed.

Of note is what appears to be a rendition of 'nose art' appearing in the form of artwork depicting an attractive woman astride a motorcycle painted on the forward panel of the machine. The vehicle's markings also feature the iconic German military insignia associated with the Iron Cross – the image derived from the original Maltese Cross, which was itself a variation of the thirteenth-century Teutonic 'cross pattée.'

The insignia was introduced in medal form in 1813 as a Prussian decoration for bravery by King Friedrich Wilhelm II during the War of Liberation against Napoleon. It came back into use in 1870 during the Franco-Prussian War and was used again in 1914 during the First World War by German Emperor Wilhelm II, before being re-introduced by Hitler with the addition of the central mounted swastika after the invasion of Poland in 1939.

Snow-Bike
During 1936 BMW apparently experimented with a new tracked motorcycle, given the name *Schneekrad*, which indicates it was designed for dealing with winter environments as might be experienced on the Eastern Front.

Practical Solution
A simpler and easier mobile machine gun platform incorporating a motorcycle sidecar won over the German military planners during the inter-war Reichswehr era, the design of which was later incorporated into the Third Reich's Wehrmacht arsenal of mobile motorized strategic planning.

The Reichswehr, composed of army and naval forces, was formed after the First World War, defined by post-war restrictions on German re-armament. Following the Nazi takeover in 1933, the Reichswehr became the Wehrmacht in 1935 – the same year the Luftwaffe was formed.

First Glimpses – 'A' for Berlin

Dated 1931, a very relaxed group of Reichswehr soldiers and civilians clown around a rarely seen 1928 Opel Motoclub 500. Founded in 1863 and making sewing machines and bicycles, Opel eventually became the largest world producer of bicycles. Then, in 1902 the factory, located in Rüsselheim, began building motorcycles. While it offered small displacement machines, its flagship model was the Motoclub, which came about after Opel purchased the Neander company and its advanced motorcycle designs. In 1928 a Motoclub 500SS fitted with twelve rockets blasted off in front of a crowd of 7,000, soon reaching a fiery speed of 220 km/h (125 mph). While things looked bright, due to the worldwide economic crisis Opel was sold to the US General Motors company in 1930 and General Motors decided to terminate motorcycle production.

The pivotal year in which this photo was composed found the Nazi Party still jockeying for power and dealing with internal conflicts that focused on the SA 'Brownshirts,' with its leaders calling for all-out radical revolution. Such notions interfered with Hitler's plans, so the SA leadership was later to be liquidated. Also in September 1931, Hitler's niece Gelli Raubal committed suicide with his gun due to his dictatorial control of her. Reportedly, he was so affected that he considered suicide as well. In October, a parade staged in the city of Brunswick rallied over 100,000 members of the SS, SA and the NSSK (National Socialist Motor Corps), taking six hours to pass before Hitler's podium, and signalling his ascension to power.

Change of Clothing/Change of Uniforms

A group of older soldiers, several wearing First World War decorations, pose for their portraits with what appears to be a showroom–condition Zündapp now serving in Germany's new military, the Wehrmacht, consisting of ground, air and naval forces. The highly theatrical and now iconic Nazi-era uniforms, including the black worn by the dreaded SS, were devised by the famous clothing design house of Hugo Boss.

Motorcycles of the Wehrmacht

Luftwaffe troops aboard a BMW R-12

Notations on the photo indicate the location was Detmold in the North Rhine-Westphalia area of Germany. The city developed a modest civilian airport project in the early 1930s that expanded into a military airfield in late 1934, and by 1935 provided hangars and barracks for Luftwaffe personnel. In addition to training facilities, the base was involved with the production of the Focke-Wulf TA154 Moskito nightfighter, an aircraft in large part made from wood as the result of the area's furniture industry. For some reason the base was never bombed. Post-war, it was taken over for use by US and British air forces.

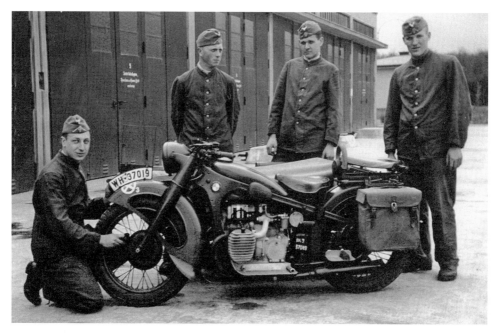

Recently Enlisted

A team of motor pool mechanics, wearing their denim work fatigues, stand with a 'minty' looking BMW R-12 (first introduced in 1939) showing its distinctive front fender. The fender carries a registration plate with the letters 'WH', indicating that the bike was the property of the Wehrmacht-Heer – Nazi Germany's army.

This is the military version that saw the civilian model's round riding pegs replaced with flat aluminium floorboards for easier placement of army boots. A popular BMW military design, and one of the most prolific, some 36,000 were ultimately built in both solo and sidecar combination.

Handstand

When a camera appeared, one acrobatically inclined mechanic could not resist the opportunity to demonstrate his athletic skills. The painted insignia on the BMW's front fender identifies the machine as belonging to the 13th Panzer Division. After 1943, the fender-mounted license plates disappeared and the machines were built with special hand and foot warming apparatus – a life-saving boon to troops facing the sub-zero Russian winters.

Preparing for Maneuvers
Within the grounds of their *kaserne* (barracks), a contingent of sidecar troops musters for a photo prior to joining a large convoy of other vehicles. One soldier holds traffic signal pennants and all are wearing goggles for eye protection and wear strapped around their necks the ubiquitous gas mask canister – a vestige of the First World War and resulting fears of chemical warfare.

Puch Pilot
With paperwork clamped between his teeth, a courier sets out on his Puch 350GS, the 347cc twin cylinder in production during 1938–42, with some 2,500 being made.

The military censors have obscured the license number and signage as the photo was used for a commercial postcard.

Along with the Austrian-made Puch, smaller numbers of various other motorcycle brands found themselves in Wehrmacht service, either built in Germany and its occupied territories or captured after battle. Those included the German-made Ardie, Horex, Kolumbus, Phanomen and Tornax; the Czechoslovakian CZ; the Polish Sokol; the Danish Nimbus; the Belgian FN, Gillet-Herstal and Sarolea; the French Gnome et Rhône, Peugeot, Terrot and Motobecane as well as various British motorcycles.

Triple Threat
A trio of Luftwaffe soldiers sit astride identical military-issue BMWs. The man on the right shows corporal's stripes (*obergefreiter*) while his companions wear their denim fatigues to protect their uniforms.

Opposite: **A Firm Grip**
A motorcycle courier appears on a commercially produced postcard, illustrated by popular Third Reich-approved artist Wolfgang Willrich and bearing his distinctive 'W' signature.

While an art student, Willrich took part in the First World War and as a corporal was decorated with the Iron Cross. While a prisoner of the French he began sketching, his drawings subsequently being spotlighted by the International Red Cross in various POW publications. Returning post-war to his school studies, he proved a top student in biology, anthropology and anatomy. In the late 1920s he was already drawing famous German generals and also began illustrating 'Nordic ethnic' types, eventually following the directions of the Nazi Party's Racial Policies Department.

Obsessively 'anti-modern', Willrich earned the support of the Nazi leadership with his portrayals of the 'heroic and racially correct' Aryan civilian and soldier. Although never joining the Party or accepting an SS position as offered by Himmler, he instead preferred to maintain his 'artistic independence'. However, Willrich was one of the organisers of the infamous Munich exhibition of so-called Degenerate Art and even considered the Nazi Party too soft on the racial subject.

If Heinrich Hoffman was Nazi Germany's 'official photographer' then Willrich could be considered the Third Reich's 'official illustrator.' During the war, Willrich, having petitioned Rommel for the opportunity, travelled extensively with German forces through France, Poland, Norway, Finland and Russia. While actively sketching portraits of the high-ranking as well as the lowly foot soldier or *landser*, he also focused on submariners and naval personnel as well as the elite airborne *Fallschirmjäger* paratroopers. In 1944 he was commissioned to prepare an illustrated book titled *That's Why the German Soldier Fought*. The war ended prior to publication and Willrich found himself transported to an American POW camp in Normandy, France, where he set about sketching GIs for extra money. Eventually, he managed to have his book published after the war in Buenos Aires. Released from captivity in 1946, he returned to his wife and three children in Goettingen. In declining health, one of his last works was an anti-war mural for his former high school. In October 1948, at age fifty-one, he succumbed to cancer. His large body of military drawings still garners considerable attention for a variety of reasons, the images having appeared on thousands of commercially produced postcards during the twelve years of the Third Reich.

Civilian Life – Lull Between the Wars

Pre-war Germany – DKW Family Transportation
Motorcycles were a popular form of both transportation and sport in pre-Third Reich Germany.
Here, family and friends pose proudly with a 1935 DKW SB500, a baby perched on its gleaming
tank. The 'IVB' prefix on the fender-mounted license frame indicates the scene is somewhere in
the Baden district (Heidelberg, Mannheim, Karlsruhe, Freiburg, Lake Constance). The SB500, a
two-stroke twin-cylinder, produced 15 hp and was manufactured between 1934 and 1939. Top
speed via a three-speed transmission was 102 km/h (62 mph).

Opposite: **Sunday Cruise**
A sporty, upscale couple cruising aboard a chrome-tanked DKW. It's interesting to note that
often neither civilian nor military riders wore gloves, at least in warmer weather.

Imported Swedish Motorcycle – Family Treasure

The registration plate indicates the photo was taken in the city of Ulm in the Württemberg area of south-eastern Germany. The centrepiece is a Swedish-made Suecia with its beautifully contoured and polished fuel tank. Built in the city of Örkelljunga, it was produced between 1928 and 1940 and was often powered by high quality British-made JAP and other engines of up to 750cc displacement. The motorcycles proved themselves in competition, resulting in a large order placed by the Swedish military; however, the outbreak of the war brought production to an end.

Ulm, situated on the River Danube and 60 miles from the Alps, is known for having the tallest church steeple in the world, which is a Gothic structure. Its history is traceable back to AD 850 and the city is also the birth place of Albert Einstein.

Constructed on the city's nearby Kuberg Hill, a concentration camp for political prisoners operated from 1933 to 1935. Ulm's 500 Jewish residents came under persecution and their synagogue was destroyed after Kristallnacht in November 1938. During the war, the city was subject to only one bombing attack. On 17 December 1944, the RAF targeted two large truck factories, destroying both along with the Gallwitz Barracks, several military hospitals and fourteen other Wehrmacht structures. Civilian casualties included 707 Ulm inhabitants while 25,000 were left homeless and over 80 per cent of the medieval city centre was reduced to rubble.

Touring in Style
Dapper pre-war motorcyclists enjoy riding a DKW along a well-paved Hanover roadway. In the distance other riders can be glimpsed as a pedestrian, visible in the background, takes in the impromptu parade.

Stuttgart Riders
A group of leather-clad civilian riders, including two young children wearing custom helmets, are enjoying the day cruising around the Stuttgart area.

As the Third Reich sharpened its manufacturing talons for war production, restraints were placed upon the German motorcycle industry. Late in 1938 the 150 different brands that were then being produced were reduced to thirty. In addition, the production of parts was drastically cut. For example, motorcycle seat options fell from twenty-two to three. Of the original twenty-five types of electric horns, now only one was available. Choices of wheels dropped from 150 to nine. While variety suffered, efficiency and economy benefited, at least for the military. However, motorcycle production plummeted in 1944 when the Wehrmacht found that their VW *Kübelwagen* (the German version of the American Jeep), though somewhat underpowered, was better suited to their needs, as well as being less expensive and easier to manufacture.

Ice Skaters

A group of young *bon vivants* have ventured out in the snow, apparently one riding his motorcycle. Notations on the reverse of the photo list the names of Franz, Rudi, Josi and Otto. The license plate indicates a Berlin registration.

DKW on the Road to France – Pre-war Tourist

The sign points in the direction of the Pont du Rhin bridge spanning the Danube and toward the city of Strasbourg some 33 km (20 miles) further on, close to the German border. As the capital of the Alsace region in eastern France, Strasbourg was evacuated of its residents at the outbreak of the war. After the German occupation of France in June 1940, the Alsace region was absorbed into the German Reich, but only its German-speaking Alsatian residents (*Volksdeutsche*) were allowed to return. All Jews were expelled and the main synagogue, a cultural and architectural landmark, was destroyed. From 1943 the city suffered further damage when it came under Allied bombing. It was eventually liberated by Free French forces on 23 November 1944.

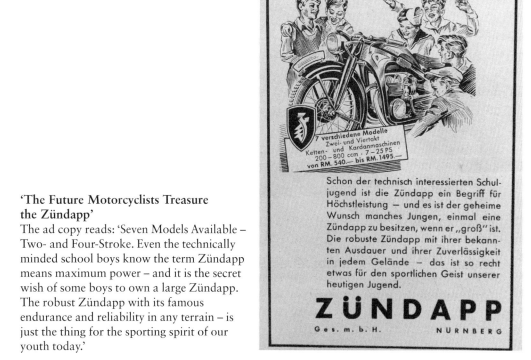

'The Future Motorcyclists Treasure the Zündapp'

The ad copy reads: 'Seven Models Available – Two- and Four-Stroke. Even the technically minded school boys know the term Zündapp means maximum power – and it is the secret wish of some boys to own a large Zündapp. The robust Zündapp with its famous endurance and reliability in any terrain – is just the thing for the sporting spirit of our youth today.'

Rare Machine?

While this is more likely a KS 500, it may be one of only 170 KKS 500 Zündapps produced between 1936 and 1938, the first model to feature foot gear-change. It was placed on the right side, with the rear brake actuated by the heel of the foot, thereby requiring some advanced coordination as both gear-change and braking were accomplished by the same foot. Its performance advantage came about due to its 498cc engine, as found in the KS 500; the motor was then placed in the much lighter DK200 frame, which originally held a 298cc engine. The apparently well-pleased rider has stopped somewhere on a rural roadway near Dresden. The machine has been raised onto its heavy-duty centre stand for the photo op. Today, it is estimated that only eight KKS 500s still exist.

Pomeranian Boy on Zündapp

Wearing traditional Tyrolean attire, the boy proudly sits astride what appears to be a 1920s 250cc single-cylinder machine.

Zündapp, established in Nuremberg in 1917, initially made fuses for artillery shells during the First World War. By 1933 the company had produced 100,000 motorcycles, then released the KS 600 in 1938. The 28 hp opposed twin was subsequently produced for the Wehrmacht from 1938 to 1941, then replaced by the Zündapp KS 750 sidecar combination, some 18,000 being purpose-built for German military use. In addition there was the K 800, the only four-cylinder motorcycle fielded by the Wehrmacht during the war.

Opposite above: IIH for Pomerania

A couple has their photo taken aboard a motorcycle registered in Pomerania. The DKW, apparently a 198cc Volksrad ES 200 single-cylinder, is equipped with an optional squeeze horn mounted at the handlebars.

Opposite below: Reappearance of DKW IIH-659

Though resurfacing many years apart, this photo appears to show the same motorcycle, minus the squeeze horn, looking a bit more worn and now with two young girls aboard, possibly the children of the couple previously seen. The motorcycle is still licensed in Pomerania.

History has long decided the fate of the historical region of Pomerania as it lies on the Baltic Sea between Germany and Poland. The area contains the pivotal port city of Danzig, annexed by Nazi Germany in 1939, which was part of the Polish Corridor that allowed Poland access to the sea. Both its Jewish and Polish population were persecuted and deported, making way for German resettlement; they in turn were expelled with significant loss of life by Soviet forces after the war ended.

Sisters from the Sudetenland

This photo of two young sisters on what appears to be a Victoria was taken in April 1936. Notations on the reverse indicate the location was the town of Hannsdorf, also known as Hanusovice in the Czech language. Prior to the war, most of its 3,351 residents were German. The reverse also bears a stamp indicating it was processed in the city of Freiwaldau by a photographer identified as Wilfried Niemetz. Freiwaldau, like Hannsdorf (Hanusovice), also lay within the Sudetenland, an area of Czechoslovakia with some 3 million German-speaking residents, which was annexed by Hitler in 1938. During the years of Nazi occupation, the Gross-Rosen concentration camp was located near Hannsdorf, while Freiwaldau was the site of another notorious camp, Thomasdorf. After the war, the Czechs and Russians forcibly expelled the ethnic German population as part of a mass exodus that resulted in hundreds of thousands of deaths while many more *Volksdeutsche* civilians were imprisoned and badly mistreated in Czech concentration and labour camps after the war.

All-Weather Riders and a Gathering Storm
Civilian bicycles and motorcyclists share a wet country road. Sidecars were an important means of family transportation as an economical substitute for cars both in Europe and the US during the early decades of the twentieth century. Eventually, many motorcycles would be 'drafted' into the war effort.

New Rider
A Luftwaffe corporal stands by an army trooper aboard a civilian 1930s DKV Luxus 200 (198cc single) showing a Posen (Poland) registration. Note the accessory speedometer coupling on the front fork leg.

Hi-Jinks
A young boy wearing a perplexed expression has been placed in the foreground of a group of clowning young *soldaten* employing a BMW sidecar as their photo prop. As the motorcycle wears a canvas black-out covering and the soldiers have their 'overseas' caps, the location may be France.

Makeshift Hitler Youth and Motorcycle
A boy in a mishmash of civilian knickers and military gear poses in front a BMW with sidecar somewhere in the area of Munich.

Motorized HJ

Dressed in their black winter uniforms, Hitler Jugend boys move up from bicycles to motorcycles. One of the perks of membership and more appealing than academic studies or church services, it was a motivation well thought out by the Nazi leadership. Hitler Youth organization motorized units included some 108,000 members by 1938. Eventually, many would be making a quantum leap to motorcycles mounted with machine guns.

1937, Bad Oyenhausen – 'I will not forget'

An HJ member wears the uniform of the naval division while his young lady friend has donned his cap. The DKW SB200 carries a Westphalia registration plate, the photo printed at a studio in Bad Oyenhausen sometime during the fourth year of the Third Reich. Handwriting on the obverse reads *Das vergess ich nicht*. Whether it was the boy or girl who added these words is unknown.

Bad Oyenhausen, a North-Rhine Westphalia spa resort located in north-west central Germany, lays claim to a world-famous thermal carbonating saltwater fountain. Named the Jordansprudel, it can reportedly spout some 125 feet into the air and provide medicinal relief. During the era of the Third Reich it hosted a gathering of the Confessing Church, one of the few religious organisations that spoke out against Nazi brutality. The town was chosen for a tank factory and was subsequently bombed on 30 March 1945. At war's end, it came under British jurisdiction, hosting the British Army of the Rhine headquarters until 1954 when it was relinquished back to local control.

'Horex – Quality Motorcycles perfectly designed and constructed – Fast, Racy and Reliable'
While the Horex depicted in the advertisement bears a Berlin area license plate, the machines were manufactured near Frankfurt, in the city of Bad Homburg. The company was founded in 1923 by the Rex glassware company, hence the name Horex. Initially developing 250cc machines, in 1933 the company introduced high-quality 600cc and 800cc parallel twin models.

Inappropriate Riding Gear on Horex
The 'IT' registration on what appears to be a 1930s Type S6 600cc single-cylinder Horex indicates the photo scene was somewhere in the vicinity of Hessen-Nassau and the city of Frankfurt. Note the belt-driven generator for the 25 hp machine's headlamp.

Horex Militarized

A soldier prepares to refuel a model T5 C1M, a 500cc single-cylinder machine now wearing its Luftwaffe registration plate and grey-green paint as well as accessory leather saddlebags. Note the sporty 'Brooklands' style exhaust. It's apparently excellent-looking condition indicates it may not have seen active battlefield service as of yet. The fuel container entered the global lexicon as 'Jerry can' after millions of them were found during the North African campaigns pitting German panzers against British and American tanks.

Softig Zündapp

As an army NCO looks on, an auxiliary female *helferinn* dons his cap and sits astride a Zündapp.

'Mutti'

A soldier has snapped a photo of his mother along with a Luftwaffe soldier aboard what appears to be a shiny new DKW SB350. Note the transmission's hand-shifter on the side of the polished alloy fuel tank. The machine still wears civilian registration for Braunschweig (Brunswick); the city is located in Lower Saxony, north of the Harz Mountains. During the Nazi era, it was a major centre for the German arms industry with its subsequent mass slave labour as well as a centre for several state institutions including the SS-Junker School and the garrison city for the 31st Infantry Division, which was instrumental in the invasion of Poland and France.

Ausgeseichnet Seitenwagen – Steib Sidecar of Nuremberg

While founded in 1914 by Josef Steib, the Nuremberg company did not begin sidecar production until prompted by an order from the Ardie motorcycle company, eventually becoming the largest sidecar producer in Germany. The advertisement reads: 'The sidecar of reputation, designed by experienced professionals, its high quality put to the test for many years.' Most sidecars in use by the German Wehrmacht were produced by Steib.

Swabian Fuel Stop for Club Members – Germany's First Petrol Station

In the district of Swabia, a pair of Reichswehr (pre-Third Reich) navy personnel are joined by young civilians at a BP (British Petroleum) OLEX refuelling station – perhaps the very first of its kind. As the young lady fills the petrol tank of the 1920s American-made Indian motorcycle, her civilian companion holds a glass container of fuel, the manner in which it was sold previously via some 2,500 pharmacies, bicycle shops, hotels and restaurants prior to the introduction of hose-equipped mechanized pumps as seen here. Their bomb-shaped sidecar sports the souvenir badges and decals of several motorcycle enthusiast organizations and rally events.

OLEX, founded in 1904, was initially an Austrian-Hungarian petroleum corporation and was the predecessor of the German subsidiary of BP, later headquartered in Berlin. It is credited with establishing in 1922 the very first purpose-built public petrol station in Germany, located near Hanover. By 1935 OLEX operated over 6,000 fuel pumps. Then with Germany on war production footing, it was folded into the *Arbeitsgemeinschaft Mineralölverteilung* fuel and mineral directorate as an officially designated Third Reich armaments company. The role played by fuel, and its diminishing supply, would take centre stage as a key factor in bringing the motorized Wehrmacht to a grinding halt.

When the Third Reich claimed sovereignty over an area of Antarctica they renamed it Neu-Schwabenland in honour of Swabia, which was both a widespread language and historical area of south-western Germany. It was home to many notables including Erwin Rommel of Afrika Korps fame as well as Claus von Stauffenberg, the leader of the failed assassination attempt against Hitler.

Sternfahrt Zeit

As the 'starting point' banner in the background indicates, riders and passengers have gathered for a motorcycle rally sometime in the early 1930s (sport motorcycling attracting thousands of adherents across Germany). They may have motored in from distant parts of the country: one visible registration plate indicates the motorcycle arrived from the Saar region, a heavily industrialised and strategically coal-rich area that after the First World War was given over as a protectorate under the League of Nations, then re-incorporated into Nazi Germany in 1935 as the Gau of Saar-Palatinate, before being re-designated as the Western Boundary of the Greater Reich (Westmark) in 1942. As a consequence of its importance to war production, it was heavily bombed by the Allies during the war.

Committed Competitors

On a stormy day in Germany, wearing then state-of-the-art safety helmets, goggles and tailored leathers, a large gathering of intrepid civilian riders prepare for a competitive event. Their elegant Model S502 Steib sidecars wear racing number plates while one rider carries a transparent map case across his chest, no doubt mapping the rally route.

No. 239
In a photo dated 1936, off-road racing takes a sidecar registered in Stuttgart into the rough. Helmet insignia indicate that the riders are members of the military.

Ende der Internationalen Sechstagefahrt:
4 Mannschaftswettbewerbe —
4 deutsche Siege.

Die 17. Motorrad-Sechstagefahrt hat von 248 Teilnehmern 130 das Ziel erreichen lassen. Zum dritten Male gewann die BMW-Nationalmannschaft Henne, Stelzer und Kraus (rechts Kraus und Seitenwagenfahrer Müller) trotz der unvorhergesehenen Zwischenfälle die internationale Trophäe.

Die DKW-Fahrer (von links) Winkler, Kluge und Geiß erfochten die Silbervase. Winkler hielt trotz einer Fußverletzung bis ans Ende durch.

Serie 1108 ad 18.9.35 Bild 4   Foto Pressebilderdienst: Schirner   Aktueller Bilderdienst, Verlag J. J. Weber, Leipzig.

'International Six Day Trails: 4 Team Events – 4 German Victories'
This official press release touts the four victories of the German national teams during the 1935 Six-Day International Trials competitions involving 248 competitors, of which only 130 succeeded in reaching the end of the gruelling event. For the third time, the BMW National team of Henne, Stelzer and Kraus took the international trophy for Germany while the three-man DKW team of Winkler, Kluge and Geiss took the silver medal, with Winkler 'holding out until the end despite a crash-related foot injury'.

Victory Celebration
As a cameraman records the moment, Ernst Jakob Henne shares the spotlight with the leader of the Third Reich as members of the National motorcycle team receive congratulations on their six-day competition victories. In the early days of political campaigning Hitler himself often trundled around Germany on a motorcycle, as did Himmler.

ERNST HENNE

Celebrity Status Collector Card
Henne was a master of all racing disciplines, from short to long distances, from asphalt to rubble tracks, and for many years was the 'fastest motorcyclist' in the world. Establishing more than seventy land speed records, he was also considered a fair-minded and model sportsman on and off the track. While conscripted by the Luftwaffe, several skull fractures incurred during his car racing crashes exempted him from military service.

494 c.c. B.M.W. (ERNST HENNE)

Henne as Post-war Hero

In November 1937 Henne established a world record of 279.5 km/h (nearly 174 mph) aboard a fully enclosed, thus distinctly shaped, 500cc super-charged BMW. As Henne, translated from German, means 'hen,' it earned him the tagline of 'Henne and his egg'. The record would stand until 1951. A very successful auto racer, he would also become one of the largest post-war Mercedes-Benz dealers in Germany. In 1991, he founded, with most of his own assets, the Ernst-Jakob-Henne Foundation to support people who are innocent victims of suffering. Ernst Henne lived with his second wife in the Canary Islands from 1996 until his death in May 2005 at the age of 101.

This particular collector card was found as a perk within packs of Will's Cigarettes of London. Such cards, produced by many British and German companies, were originally called 'stiffeners' as they were intended to strengthen the package. Will's cards first appeared in 1889; the last set was printed in 1939 at the outset of the Second World War.

Into Battle

Starting Line in Austria – Starting Line for the Second World War
Joining dozens of other competitors, the rider in the foreground pilots an Italian-made flat-twin cylinder powered 500cc Moto-Guzzi. The event appears to be the staging of the 1939 International Six-Day Trials (ISDT) as the No. 55 entry seen in the background is recorded as ridden by Italian rider Palois. German riders, aboard BMW, NSU, DKW, Puch and Zündapp machines, bested the Italians for the International Trophy – one of several solo and team competition categories.

The British sent both a military team and a civilian team, the latter including BSA team riders Les Ridgeway, Fred Perks, Fred Whitehouse and the event's lone female competitor Miss Marjorie Cottle, a multi-award winning professional racer who had shared in the British Ladies' Team's win of the Six-Days International Silver Vase in 1927.

Rest Stop/Check Point for German Rider

A DKW rider sporting lucky number 7 is offered refreshment by an event volunteer while uniformed members of the NSKK, the paramilitary vehicle organization, acting as timing officials for the event, log in the competitor's arrival. Several children strain for a look at the rider and his motorcycle, its fender plate indicating registration in Baden.

This was the twenty-first running of the highly challenging annual event, which was first staged in 1913 and considered the 'Olympics of Motorcycling'. In 1933, the year of Hitler's rise to power, the German team won the International Trophy, repeating their win in 1934 and 1935. In 1939, following the 1938 annexation of Austria into 'Greater Germany,' the Six-Day event took place in Salzburg, Austria, between 21 and 26 August, just days prior to the German invasion of Poland on September 1.

As a result of the looming threat of war, the British civilian team, among many of the other international competitors, was ordered home by British officials in the midst of the competition. All complied with the exception of Miss Marjorie Cottle who, riding a Triumph, refused to leave and continued to compete alongside the British military team until the soldiers were ordered to leave on the fifth day of the six-day event. The group then simply rode their motorcycles the 800 miles across Austria into neutral Switzerland, then through France for shipping back to Britain. While Germany was declared the winner of the 1939 ISDT, the ruling was voided post-war by the FIM governing body. In 2013, marking the 100th anniversary of the event, 600 competitors from thirty-two nations entered into the competition staged along the 1,200-mile course.

**Vintage Toy Solider –
Polizei BMW**
A highly detailed rendering
of a 1930s BMW motorcycle
as ridden by a member of
the civilian police wearing
his distinctive green uniform
and traditional 'Shako'
style cap.

**To Protect and Serve:
Motorized Polizei**
A civilian constable, wearing
the traditional Shako helmet
and carrying a briefcase
as well as a rifle, seems to
be following a Wehrmacht
Unteroffizier (NCO) aboard
a much larger machine.
Both are wearing black-out
regulation headlamps,
which indicates that the
scene is during the war
years but most likely in
Germany itself, as indicated
by the policeman in
civilian uniform.

NSKK Motorcycle Police aboard BMWs in Bavaria.
Special motorcyclist training was carried out by the NSKK, the National Socialist Motorized Corps. Between 1933 and 1939, the NSKK provided 187,000 trained vehicle drivers to the German military.

Balancing Act
Demonstrating their skills on what may be a local school's running track, NSKK riders perform for an audience of Hitler Youth.

Motorized Police – Rhineland Re-Occupied
A group of Border Customs Protection Service soldiers, equipped with a DKW sidecar and armed with what appears to be the 9 mm MP28 sub-machine gun as well as the motorcycle-mounted British Bren gun or Czech variation machine gun, pose somewhere in the Rhineland, as indicated by the license plate on their automobile. In violation of the Versailles Treaty, Nazi Germany re-occupied the Rhineland region on 7 March 1936.

Opposite above: **Traffic Control**
Vehicles are being redirected for some unknown reason, perhaps due to an accident, an event route or the arrival of VIPs. A civilian model 1931 DKW stands in the background, with a picnic thermos perched on the rear passenger seat. Its license plate prefix 'IS' indicates a Stuttgart registration.

Stuttgart, located in southern Germany, was given the honorary title 'The City of Germans living Outside of the Reich'. Its Jewish population was deported to Riga, Latvia, with only 180 surviving. During 1944 American and British bombing raids destroyed most of the central city – the three raids claiming 4,477 civilian lives. Eventually, the city was occupied by Allied forces, who encountered little resistance.

Opposite below: **Accident Investigation**
Civilian police examine the wreckage of an NSU that may have failed to negotiate the curve or collided with an oncoming vehicle as its front forks are mangled. The registration plate places the scene in the Hamburg area.

Military Policeman

A DKW SB500 wears a *polizei* identification plate. Its rider is in civilian clothes, while what appears to be a half-track SdKfz 10 D7 Demag military truck is visible in the background.

Many military policemen came from the civilian forces of Germany's big cities, where they had previously dealt with traffic control, street crime and the often violent street demonstrations occurring during Germany's political turmoil of the 1920s. They shared their longstanding police traditions and comradeship and held the safety and security of their homeland at heart.

With the rise to power of the Nazi Party and the assimilation of the German police formations under the control of Himmler's SS, many members would fight and die in combat on both the Eastern and Western Fronts either in anti-Partisan actions or frontline engagements with Allied forces.

Some would join special execution units that would take part in 'The Holocaust by Bullets', engaging in the face-to-face murder of over 1 million men, women and children. After the war's end, many returned to their civilian police roles, concealed their complicity in the Holocaust and very few were ever brought to justice.

Shovel Soldiers

A group of RAD boys seem to enjoy having their photo taken with a DKW SB500 Luxus, identified by its dual headlamps and matched to a fashionable Steib sidecar.

The Reich Labour Service (*Reichsarbeitdienst*) or RAD was a compulsory paramilitary organization established by law in June 1934 whereby nineteen to twenty-five-year-olds, male and female, worked in the fields with farmers or performed other labour for a period of six months within a strictly disciplined program, in which they drilled as soldiers but carried spades. With it, Hitler solved the massive unemployment problems, provided cheap labour, indoctrinated the young and was also able to sidestep the restrictions of the post-First World War Versailles Treaty that sought to limit German military expansion. In effect, RAD was a means to transition German youth into a military mould for later incorporation into the various branches of the Wehrmacht.

RADman on DKW

Flowers decorate the headlamp of the young paramilitary recruit who will be exchanging his RT100 Standard for a shovel. The smallest and also the most popular DKW, the two-stroke single-cylinder engine of 97cc displacement could reach 43 mph. The economical machine featured a three-speed gearbox, weighed only 119 lb and sipped petrol at 140 miles per gallon.

RAD at Speed

A Labour Service member demonstrates both a sense of balance and bravado as he stands in the seat of a sidevalve BMW moving at speed through the countryside. The license plate indicates registration in Stuttgart.

RAD recruits entered a regimen that emphasised 'classlessness' – all members ostensibly being graded on performance rather than their socio-economic status or level of education while strict adherence to the rules and submersion of self into the *uberkorpf* of the Third Reich was demanded en masse.

Willi Playing 'Tom Mix' in Potsdam – Photo Dated 1936

In this pre-war photo, a 'spiess', or master sergeant, pretends to hold a rifle as he clowns for the camera while aboard a BMW, the transmission hand-shift lever of which is visible on the right side of the petrol tank.

Spiess translates to 'pike' or 'spear' and was the common German soldier's nickname for the almost all-powerful master sergeant, in this case one who signed his name as Willi. Additional written notations on this Berlin-printed photo-postcard find the writer comparing himself to Tom Mix, the American cowboy film star long popular with German audiences. Mix, known as the 'King of Cowboys', earned a vast fortune from his 336 films but would die in 1940, four years after this photo was taken, at the age of sixty during a high-speed car crash in Arizona when his heavy suitcase full of money and jewels struck his head.

Directly bordering Berlin, Potsdam would serve as the location of the post-war Potsdam Conference conducted by Churchill, Truman and Stalin, who gathered there nine weeks after Nazi Germany's surrender to decide the goals of the post-war occupation of the divided country.

Cover Story

The 15 February 1939 copy of the official Wehrmacht magazine featured a dramatic cover shot of a BMW R4, the less than potent but very reliable single-cylinder machine somehow managing to leap over a hill – an image certain to attract a reader's attention.

The issue contained a profile on the various Luftwaffe districts within Germany, an article concerning horses as well as a feature on lesser-known mechanized military vehicles including variations of the Kettenkrad (SdFz2) tracked transporter. Articles also showcased the new Volkswagen 'people's car' plus a travel correspondent's visit to Hawaii's Pearl Harbor, some two years prior to the Japanese attack and America's entry into the Second World War.

Similar Themed Postcard Perfect

One of a series of 'Our Army' themed commercial postcards printed by the Kosmos company shows a BMW R11 ascending a hill on its rear wheel, making for a striking silhouette. While published after the take-over of the Nazi Party and the official name change of the military from Reichswehr to Wehrmacht, the motorcycle shows the Reichswehr registration.

Sidecar Experts

During field training exercises, both solo and sidecar machines traverse a variety of terrains, the location of the photo being somewhere in the eastern German state of Prussia. The numerous dents appearing on the machines indicate the seriousness of the exercises.

Prepared for the Elements

Another training session finds the motorcycle troops outfitted in sheepskin coats as they travel via a BMW 750cc R11 sidecar outfit and a Type 40 Light Uniform Personnel Vehicle on a winter's day in Germany. The motorcycle's license plates still bear the RW designation of the pre-Third Reich Reichswehr although the soldiers wear the uniform of the new regime. Appearing in 1932, the R11 was the first time BMW's sidevalve, flat-twin engine was couched in a pressed steel frame. The motorcycles proved more durable than the Type 40, which was eventually replaced in 1938 by the versatile Kübelwagen, similar to the US Jeep.

Ice Fantasy
Motorcycle troopers negotiate a snowy landscape in January 1940, several months after the invasion of Poland and six months prior to the summertime invasion of France.

Casual Conversations
Officers, one still wearing his riding goggles around his neck, pause for a cigarette. In the background, a Zündapp KS 500 motorcycle's steel wheel shares the scene with the wooden spoked wheels of a horse-drawn wagon, whose numbers far outweighed the motorized weaponry of the Wehrmacht. The wagon appears to be loaded with a jumble of rifles, perhaps confiscated French weapons.

Heavy Freight
A sidevalve BMW R11 contrasts sharply against the large hulks of army transport vehicles showing WH designation. The rider wears a soft visor cap from early in the war along with his denim fatigue trousers. Note the machine's heavy-duty front fender braces and fork support.

Idyllic Composition
German soldiers, joined by a motorcycle painted in winter white camouflage, have gathered farm animals somewhere in Russia. A young boy seems to be assisting them, cradling a piglet. Initially well-received by the Ukrainians as they entered Soviet territory, German troops were welcomed as liberators from Stalin's iron yoke. In reality the Third Reich stripped all its occupied territories, particularly in the east, of almost all livestock and food supplies, in part to feed their troops in the field, but also as part of a systematic programme to starve to death some 30 million Russian civilians in order to make *lebensraum* for the new German masters of the land.

Antics
To identify himself in the photo for later reference, a Zündapp-riding motorcycle trooper has circled himself.

Improvised Sidecar
The special vulcanised protective coats of the *kradmelder* are clearly visible as BMW-riding motorcycle troops clown for the camera, the baby carriage not a far cry from their sidecars.

'War Year 1941'
A motorcycle trooper has recorded his year of service, inking it onto a photo of himself and his crew aboard a BMW R12 matched to a BMW-badged sidecar. The year began well enough for German war planners, with the summer seeing the invasion of the Soviet Union and initial successes with rapid advances and whole Russian armies captured, but by the end of the year, once encountering stiffening Russian resistance and the vastness of the country, Germany found itself for the first time on the defensive.

Rest Stop in France
A detachment of Luftwaffe motorcycle troops stop for a break on the grounds of a Chevrolet car dealership.

No Smiles for the Camera
Wearing the now-iconic *stahlhelm* steel helmets, in this case showing the national tri-colour decal that would later be replaced by Third Reich insignia, pre-war troops pause during training. An NSU 500 OSL is seen at the lead.

Czechoslovakia – 15 March 1939 – German Troops Occupy the Country
Motorcycle troops riding BMWs with SS identification plates of the Leibstandarte SS take part in a parade through the city of Prague.

Czechoslovakia had been 'given' to Nazi Germany by Britain and France to appease Hitler, who had promised that he had no further territorial ambitions. While the area carved out of the country, the Sudetenland, was home to 3 million ethnic Germans (thus Hitler's claim to the area), the agreement also gave over the majority of the country's coal, iron, steel and electrical power resources. While Germany gained the Sudetenland in October 1938, without a shot fired; five months later Hitler would take the rest of the country, once again without meeting international resistance, thus emboldening him for further conquests by force. Poland would be next in the cross-hairs.

Dog Day Afternoon
Greeted with flowers and a friendly dog, smiling SS men meet no resistance as they take over a country without firing a shot, at least initially. Terror soon followed for the occupied Czechs.

While the Leibstandarte Adolf Hitler (LSSAH) was initially an elite bodyguard unit serving Hitler, it also functioned as an honour guard and security detail at the annual Nazi Party rallies at Nuremberg. It took part in the 1935 German re-occupation of the Saarland as well as the initial occupation of the Sudetenland in 1938. By 1939, the LSSAH was a full infantry regiment fielding three infantry battalions, an artillery battalion as well as combat engineers, anti-tank and reconnaissance units including motorcycle troops. It later took on a combat role in Poland and the USSR, eventually becoming a panzer (mechanized) division. Members of the LSSAH were also complicit in the murder of least 5,000 POWs, mostly Soviet troops on the Russian Front, and were judged guilty of war crimes by the post-war Nuremberg Tribunal.

Hunters' Hearts
A trio of *kradmantel*-wearing *kradschützen*; one is wielding the iconic MP38/40 sub-machine gun and the two corporals are strapped with the standard messenger satchel.

New Perspective
A motorcycle trooper carries his Mauser carbine slung over his left shoulder while his gas mask canister rests against his chest. The latter equipment was initially made mandatory as the result of poison gas use during the First World War by both the German and Allied forces. The battlefield use of gas did not occur during Second World War, being reserved instead for the Nazi death camps.

Cover of *Der Adler*
The Eagle, a bi-weekly illustrated magazine, was published in Berlin with the participation of the Reich Air Ministry. First appearing on 1 March 1939, it continued in print until 12 September 1944.

This 21 January 1941 issue featured a drawing by war correspondent Ellgaard depicting a Luftwaffe motorcyclist deploying flight crews to their bombers. At this point, Germany was waging war against England with its aerial blitzkrieg of London and other British cities. While Operation Barbarossa was being planned, the invasion of the Soviet Union would not take place until late June, the date being delayed due to Mussolini's troops being routed in his failed invasion of the Balkans and Greece, with Hitler again diverting troops to his aid.

The Beer Lives On
Somewhere in the German state
of Saxony, soldiers and civilians
have their photo taken in front of
a guest house and beer parlour.
Joining them on the muddy street
is a well-worn civilian-plated NSU
OSL351.

Part of the visible restaurant's
signage refers to Wolters Hofbrau,
a famous 380-year-old brewery
located in the city of Brunswick
in Lower Saxony. In 1943 Allied
bombing of the city nearly
destroyed the brewery, but it was
rebuilt in 1949 and today it is a
modern and prosperous privately
owned company offering half a
dozen different brews.

**Popular Enthusiast Magazine –
Popular Zündapp KS 750**
With a publication date one day
after Christmas 1942, the cover
illustration of *Das Motorrad*
has a decidedly martial tone.
Inside, articles cover technical
matters as well as a photo
feature concerning Ernst Henne's
motorcycle speed records. While
there are photos from the North
African campaign including
Rommel's 'strategic retreat' from
General Montgomery's British 8th
Army, there is no mention of the
disaster then befalling the German
6th Army at Stalingrad.

Transformation
A team of Army motor pool mechanics poses with a NSU newly minted in Wehrmacht grey trim,
its civilian chrome gleam now subdued.

Contemplating Repairs
A mechanic ponders his next step in what appears to be a complete engine rebuild for a single-cylinder DKW NZ350. When the DKW NZ350 models were designated for employment by the military, its first gear transmission ratio was reduced from civilian specs to match the slower marching speed of troops.

Balancing Act
A motor pool crew checks over a sidecar outfit still bearing Frankfurt area civilian registration numbers. The photo is dated 1936 – three years after Hitler's rise to power, and three years prior to Germany's attack on Poland.

Convoy Maintenance Station
A team of fatigue-wearing mechanics tend to an NSU 250ZDB. In the background a long line of heavy trucks and an officer's command car are parked during a break in a maneuver exercise. Note the leather saddlebags, black-out covers over the headlamps, monochrome paint and Wehrmacht registration plates.

Roadside Repairs
The soldier seems to be in good cheer despite the condition of his very dilapidated machine, which appears to be a Czech-made 175cc CZ. He's removed his uniform jacket and rolled up his sleeves to install a new rear wheel and tire. Notations on the reverse indicate the location is on France's defensive Maginot Line, which the German invasion bypassed in its lightning defeat of French forces. Motor troops were trained and expected to be able maintain and make repairs on their own machines as they were often in the field and far from a mechanics' station.

Elegant Attire
Wearing his pre-war, and later discontinued, dress 'walking-out' uniform or *waffenrock*, a soldier sits astride a civilian model NSU 351 OSL complete with dual airhorns. The IK designation indicates a point of registration in the Schlesien province (now in Poland).

Special Sport BMW
A requisitioned civilian BMW R66 has had its front fender hand-lettered with 'WH', indicating it is now enlisted in the German Army, but it has not been given its military cloak of grey paint. Its rider – perhaps its original owner, also now drafted in service – wears a corporal's chevron on his uniform sleeve and carries a leather messenger's pouch. The 'IID' license plate worn by the truck in the background indicates the location is Bavaria, perhaps Baden.

The R66, introduced as a 1938 model, featured new a plunger-type rear suspension and a tubular frame rather than the pressed steel frame of previous BMW models. The 597cc high-performance engine powered the company's first pre-war sporting motorcycle and set a new standard of excellence.

Taking the Stairs
A *gefreiter* (corporal) in early pre-war uniform
manoeuvres a lightweight Miele down a stone
stairway. The tank-shifting, single-cylinder
Sachs-powered machine was produced from
1932 to 1940 in Gütersloh, Germany. Various
models ranged in displacement from 60, 74, 98
and 198cc. Note the black-out headlamp.

Impromptu Performance
Somewhere in occupied France, a grandstanding soldier pilots a high-piped British-made
Matchless – perhaps the spoils of war. Off-road competitions and stunt motorcycling events
were popular in pre-war Germany, with many talented riders soon finding themselves, and their
bikes, in Wehrmacht grey.

Matchless Repairs
A soldier, enjoying the summer sun, inspects the exhaust pipe of another Matchless, in this case a 350cc single-cylinder G3. The headlamp cover is marked with a 'G', which could indicate the soldier is a member of the motorized division led by General Heinz Guderian that had operated so successfully in the French campaign, with his panzers breaking French lines at Sedan directly leading to France's surrender.

Headstand Stunt
The illustration appears on a collectible card found inside packages of Salem Zigaretten. Its caption translates to: 'Motorcyclists on Sports Day. In addition to the amazing demonstrations of motor sport today, they also can enter into battle.'

**Landlocked Sailors – Public
Demonstration at Kiel**
Uniformed Kriegsmariners serving at
the major naval base perform for fellow
military and civilians while perched on a
sidevalve BMW.

During Nazi Germany's 1930s
military expansion, the Kiel shipyards,
previously the headquarters of the
Germany Imperial Navy during the
First World War, prospered with the
construction of Kriegsmarine vessels
from battleships to submarines. Located
on the northern Baltic coast, it was also
home to the German naval academy.
Suffering some thirty-five bombing
raids during the war, 80 per cent of the
strategic city was destroyed.

Structural Integrity
A Zündapp carries extra passengers
and significantly raises the motorcycle's
centre of gravity.

Mobile Signal Post
As a soldier prepares to snap their photograph, members of the mechanized forces, wearing their distinctive black uniforms, wave swastika pennants as they perform for an audience ringing the parade ground of a military base.

Hi-Bar in Motion
Gymnastic dexterity displayed during a public demonstration of riding skills at a military base. The Zündapp K 800's 'third wheel' has been removed from the sidecar as one soldier is acting as a counterweight to the gyrations of his comrade swinging on the gymnast's high bars. The skills practiced transferred to challenges met on the battlefield.

Jumping Through Flaming Hoops for the Home Front
Members of a motorcycle troop demonstration team execute their derring-do before a large
crowd during one of many public events staged at military installations across the country.

Front Page Exhibition – Newspaper dated 19 June 1938
It is doubtful that the tattered pages carried a story about the firebombing and destruction of the
famous Munich synagogue that occurred ten days earlier on 9 June, but it most likely did publish
announcements of the newest decree; namely, one that required registration of all Jewish businesses.

Mobile Music BMW

Luftwaffe band members, wearing their distinctive *schwalbennester* or 'swallow's nest' shoulder insignia, entertain at a public exhibition. Two soldiers play accordions, which was one of the most popular instruments in Germany at the time even though the Nazi Party had tried to ban it as unbefitting German culture until composers, rallying to the instrument, began composing classical music for it. The photo appeared in the Sunday 14 March 1939 edition of the Munich newspaper *Illustrierter Beobachter* (IB), a large-format 10 x 14-inch Nazi Party publication that attracted a national audience. It contained international as well as local German news, often with propagandist swipes at the US, as well as anti-Semitic reporting.

Death Defying

Tempting fate and gravity, a stunt rider attempts to clear a speeding motorcycle as a civilian audience watches. Snapped at the instant of intersection of man and machine, the outcome is unknown.

Standing Room Only
Soldiers and a lone female civilian seeking a better view balance atop a Zündapp KS 600 sidecar combination.

Shipping Out
An NCO hefting a duffel bag and wearing his overseas cap poses for a snap with a 1939 R23 250cc single-cylinder BMW, perhaps his transportation; the location is a military post in Germany. The civilian registration plates on the machine indicate the Stuttgart area.

Leading the Way

Bogged down in French traffic during the May 1940 invasion of that country, a Zündapp KS 600 sidecar trooper checks on the progress of his comrades far back down the road, which is clogged with French civilian and German military transport.

Pathfinders – French Invasion

Twin paths in a field – one followed by a soldier on foot, smiling for the photo, the other by a weary-looking motorcycle trooper who has been wrestling his heavy mount through the dense growth. Notations for the photo read: 'Difficult advance through the wet, muddy fields near Mont-Fauxelles.' The area is located in the Ardennes region, the path the German invasion forces took in a surprise move that circumvented the vaunted Maginot Line. It was also the area, late in the war, where Hitler gambled on a last-ditch effort, attacking again through the heavily wooded area.

Victory Toast
Cycle troops pass a bottle of French champagne as the Wehrmacht sweeps through France in six weeks, liberating many of the country's famous vineyards in the process.

Sidecar Ambulance
A German motorcyclist has stopped for a souvenir photo while transporting a wounded French African colonial soldier. Inasmuch as few Germans outside the major cities had ever seen a black African, they were often viewed as a curiosity by some, while others more influenced by Nazi racist propaganda summarily executed them when captured, with several thousand dying in the defence of France, though far from their African homelands.

Eve of Destruction

Notations on the reverse of the photo identify the central figure as General of the Infantry Walther Lichel, taken in late August 1939 a few days prior to the invasion of Poland. Lichel's awards included the Knight's Cross with Swords. Two NCO adjutants stand 'at ease' beside a BMW sidecar combo.

Lichel's service record includes: 1936–38, Commanding Officer 22nd Regiment; 1938–39, General Officer Commanding 3rd Cavalry Division; 1939–40, General Officer Commanding 3rd Division; 1940–41, General Officer Commanding 123rd Division; 1941–44, Severely wounded, hospitalised and recovering, returning to service 1944–45 as General Officer Commanding Military District XI. Lichel survived the war and was kept in Allied captivity until 1947, when he was released. He passed away in 1969 at the age of eighty-four.

Besten Kampfmittel

'The best combat equipment for the best soldiers.' The BMW advert heralds the R75 750cc sidecar with an illustration of motorcycle troops in winter gear – an echo of the war being fought on the Eastern Front.

Front Row Seating on an NSU
An army trooper takes aim with his standard army issue bolt-action Mauser rifle, using a comrade's shoulder for support, who in turn relies on a sidecar for his own seating. The NSU motorcycle still shows civilian plates, indicating a recent recruitment.

Soviet-German Temporary Solidarity – 1939
Germans gather around a German-made civilian Triumph BD250 (248cc) model capable of 59 mph. It carries a license plate with the Cyrillic letters of the Russian language that translate to 'Poland'. German and Red Army forces, temporarily allied via the notorious Molotov-Ribbentrop Pact, attacked Poland from the west and east, effectively dividing the spoils, and the death and destruction, between them.

While Triumph traces its manufacture back to the late nineteenth century, until 1929 the machines were made both in Coventry, England, and Nuremberg, Germany. Though not as popular with the German military as the 350cc DKW, the German Triumph subsidiary company Triumph Werke Nurnberg produced a number of their S350 machines for the Luftwaffe.

'Triumph – used to victory and rigorously tested during many high performance competitions.'

While they bore the same ancestry and name as the famous British motorcycle, more than 12,000 of the TWN 250cc units were built under license for the Wehrmacht at the Nuremberg factory, the city that was also home to Steib sidecars, the annual Nazi Party rallies and later the post-war war Nuremberg War Crimes Tribunals.

Arrival of the Victors

In May 1940, somewhere in France, a veteran army officer wearing First World War-era battle ribbons and the Iron Cross First Class strides by a group of BMW riders (R4 on left; R35 on right). Other members of the group have noticed the cameraman as well as a French civilian woman and child caught in the middle of the scene.

French Motorcyclist POW
Captured by advancing German troops seen receding into the distance, a French soldier stands stiffly for the photograph, prompted by his captors. One of the motorcycles seen behind him may have been his machine, perhaps a Gnome et Rhône, many of which would also be captured and rebadged for Wehrmacht use.

'Here lies a brave French soldier'
Against the backdrop of a blast-splintered tree, two Mauser rifles rest against the *kradmelder*'s BMW sidecar as his comrade snaps a photo of a fallen enemy's gravesite with its respectful signage.

French Girl in German Sidecar

Wearing a perturbed expression, the passenger in the two-toned, colour-matched Steib sidecar awaits the rider of the well-maintained civilian DKW fitted with its right-hand, fuel tank-mounted gear shift. Upon the country's liberation, harsh punishment was meted out to French women who fraternised with their German occupiers.

Spokes of Another Generation

A Luftwaffe ground trooper sits proudly aboard a sleek Zündapp, the 1934–35 K 200 standing in sharp contrast to the farmer's wagon in the background. While the Third Reich presented itself as the technological avant-garde of Europe, most of its vaunted war machine rolled on wooden wheels powered by living horsepower while its troops slogged on hob-nailed boots.

New Directions

A group of soldiers gather for a souvenir photograph in France. One, carrying a messenger's leather pouch and a traffic control baton, is apparently the rider of the DKW, his Mauser rifle resting somewhat carelessly against its tank.

Employed as a middle-weight dispatch machine, the DKW NZ350 was built exclusively for the Wehrmacht as of 1941, with some 45,000 being produced.

'The Fast NSU Machines with Good Roadholding'

The NSU was another Wehrmacht warhorse, the marque's name being derived from the city of its manufacture, Neckarsulm, thus the letters NSU. The company first produced knitting machines in the early industrial age *c.* 1873, then moved on to bicycles and automobiles as well as V-twin motorcycles that rivalled the popularity of Indian, ranking second in England during the early 1900s.

Civilian NSU OSL350 and Luftwaffe Corporal

In the 1920s NSU already offered a variety of light, medium and heavy-weight motorcycles, but then in 1930 it experienced a major boost when Norton engineer Walter William Moore brought them a new 500cc engine design, launching several successful OHV engines of varying displacements including the OS and OSL models. The OSL350 seen here featured exposed valve springs, which are just noticeable where the exhaust pipe enters the engine port. The larger engined OSL500 and oSL601 were also available.

NSU from Dresden on the Eastern Front

Pausing for a drink from his canteen, a dispatch rider with his carbine slung over his back sits astride his high-piped NSU 501 OSL somewhere in Russia. Gone is the polished chrome and lustrous civilian paint, but the 12.5 hp, 65 mph machine still carries its civilian license plate, the 'II' indicating Dresden as its original home – a city destined for a fiery fate.

Sleep of the Dead
Exhausted motorcycle troops sleep in their gear, including their gas mask canisters.

Victoria as an Artform
The illustration appeared in a book published in 1928 as one of a collection of designs by famed German graphic artist Ludwig Hohlwein of Munich. A master of poster art, he created advertisement images for some 300 companies including BMW and Zeiss, as well as for the 1936 Berlin Olympics and many additional posters and billboards for Third Reich propaganda. Hohlwein joined the Nazi Party in 1933, the year of Hitler's assumption of power, becoming an officially sanctioned artist. Visiting the pre-war US, he was commissioned by Camel cigarettes for his work, but later refused an offer to emigrate to the America, preferring to continue his post-war work in a studio at Berchtesgaden, the location of Hitler's Alpine retreat, before dying in 1949 at the age of seventy-five.

V

A factory worker stands by his nicely appointed civilian Victoria KR25 motorcycle, some time between 1937 and 1940. The single-cylinder, two-stroke 247cc engine produced 9 hp, reaching speeds of 58 mph and ran at at 62 miles per gallon. Its headlamp has been covered either for black-out requirements or to protect the glass lens. Notation on the reverse of the photo indicates the photo was taken in April 1940.

Victoria Kraftrader – 'Proven in peace and war, reliable for every purpose.'
As depicted in a magazine advertisement, the larger displacement and rather sporty four-stroke, single-cylinder Victoria KR 35 SN was considered the best solo rider machine in the service of the Wehrmacht. Called the 'Engineer' in its military form, some 12,000 had been ordered by the end of the war.

Military Rider – Civilian Plates – Baden
The machine appears to be a late 1920s or
early 1930s Victoria.

D-Rad New Model Advertisement
Produced in a Spandau (Berlin) facility from
1925 to 1933 by Deutsche Industriewerke,
D-Rad (under the direction of Martin Stolle)
competed very successfully in the 1930s with
riders Franz Heck, Franz Seelos and Paul
Bulow. In 1931 the company was acquired by
NSU; the bikes, including their own line of
sidecars and sidecar taxis, were also exported
to Poland, Bohemia, Moravia, Slovakia, the
Balkans and even the Soviet Union. Some
44,500 units were built, including those
powered by a 500cc sidevalve engine of their
own design as well two-stroke powerplants
and their own versions of the 'boxer'
longitudinal-mounted engine similar to BMW
design. Models included the D-Rad Star, the
R0/4, R1/4, and L7.

Bike from Baden-Baden

A relatively rarely seen D-Rad R9 with sidecar combination bears registration plates for the Baden area, comprised of Heidelberg, Mannheim, Karlsruhe, Freiburg and Lake Constance. Its fuel tank carries the distinctive triangular-shaped nameplate. The name D-Rad consisted of Deutsche (German) and Rad, a shortening of *Motorrad* – German for motorcycle.

Poland on the Brink of the Soviet Precipice

With a train loaded with vehicles appearing in the background, a solo messenger rider aboard a Victoria is caught between two fellow soldiers, with the NCO carrying a traffic control baton tucked in his belt. Notations on the reverse of the photo state the location as Sedziszow, Poland. The captured moment in time was 25 June 1941; just four days earlier, massed German forces and their allies had invaded the Soviet Union.

Prior to the German invasion of Poland on 1 September 1939, the population of Sedzizow included 861 Jews. German police squads organised the round-up of 1,900 Jews from the town and surrounding area. During one *aktion* taking place in July 1942, 1,500 were shipped to the Belzec death camp. German soldiers also rounded up 400 Jewish residents and herded them into the Jewish cemetery. All were ordered to undress, and then were shot and buried in a mass grave. Post-war, an obelisk was erected in the Sedziszow cemetery commemorating the mass execution.

'Everywhere quickly ahead with Sachs-Motor...'
Sachs holds the distinction of being the world's oldest motorcycle manufacturer, having been founded in 1886 in Schweinfurt. The city was also a major centre for ball-bearing manufacture and was heavily bombed during the war.

Airman in the Wind
The notation on the reverse of this photo indicates it was taken in Poland on 16 September 1939, just two weeks after Germany's invasion. A major in the Luftwaffe is showing off his apparently new motorcycle – one that may be a small displacement single-cylinder two-stroke powered by a Sachs-Motor employed by several different motorcycle manufacturers.

Gebirgsjäger Goricke
A mountain trooper, wearing a ribbon in his second button hole indicating the awarding of the
Iron Cross Second Class, takes time out for a smoke and a photograph. His mount, a Goricke,
traces its history to 1903. Known initially for its racing bicycles, Goricke later became one of the
pioneering motorcycle companies of Germany. During the 1920s their 177cc to 247cc powered
machines utilized the well-known British-designed Villiers engines while their 346 and 496cc
motors were supplied by another British company, MAG. This particular machine still carries its
Bavarian civilian registration plate.

Out of Uniform
Well-equipped in fashionable motorcycling leather gear, a Hitler Youth member has donned his
HJ cap for his portrait aboard an as-yet unidentified machine.

Summer in the Steppes
A young German soldier wearing a t-shirt and shorts enjoys a ride on his DKW in the Russian sunshine. In the background can be seen a *nachrichten* (communications) truck.

DKW NZ350 as Moving Target
A motorcycle trooper was literally a moving target silhouetted against the vast emptiness of the Russian landscape. His life depended on his skill, his Mauser Kar. 7.92 mm bolt-action rifle and, in this case, his DKW motorcycle.

Metal to Metal
A German trooper aboard a DKW NZ350 poses beside a knocked-out Red Army tank, one of hundreds littering the battlefield from the Wehrmacht's early successes in 1941. But in July 1943, during the largest armoured battle in history, one that shook the earth at Kursk in the southern Ukraine, the Wehrmacht suffered an estimated 210,000 killed and wounded, while the Soviets suffered 178,000. Though considered a stalemate, it also signalled the last major German assault on the Eastern Front, with the tide of war about to sweep over the mechanized blitzkrieg as it was slowly but relentlessly thrown out of its conquered Soviet territories.

The enemy they faced including partisans, prone to stretching a virtually invisible wire or cable across a road. Pulled to neck height, a speeding motorcyclist encountering it could literally lose his head. Eventually, the motorcycles were outfitted with metal bars or rails placed vertically across and above the handlebars in an effort to counter such lethal ambushes.

DKW Sailor
Somewhere in France, a Kriegsmariner poses on perhaps a showroom-fresh DKW 494cc SB500 that now wears a black-out headlamp and a 'WM' (for Wehrmacht-Kriegsmarine) license plate.

Shore Legs
Donning his riding gloves, another Kriegsmariner trades in his ship for a BMW K71 – the model first brought out in 1938. While originally targeted for civilian consumption, it became a standard of the German army for dispatch, scouting and mobile infantry, often being fitted with a sidecar as seen here. In need of more power than its 18 hp, it was superseded in 1941 by the R75.

Bayonet Passenger
Two comrades pose aboard a BMW R35 single, in a photograph taken in 1939.

Convoy
Gas mask canisters hanging across their chests, a troop of *kradmelders* pose by their machines, with only one managing to smile for the camera.

Sidecar Artistry in Motion
An illustration of a Zündapp sidecar crew in action appears on a commercial Feldpost postcard that was popular with the troops. Note the use of the sidecar grip rail as a trooper apparently makes a fast entry on the run.

Battle Ready
During maneuvers, a BMW sidecar crew slogs through the mud. Sidecars were often equipped with a light machine gun fed by a high-capacity double drum canister, as seen here. The image was an official Wehrmacht 'press photo' that appeared on commercial postcards.

The training helped somewhat when German motorcycle troops encountered the Russian wet season and the accompanying sea of mud. Virtually quicksand, the liquid sand seeped into every cranny of their machines, destroying engines. Repair teams in the field struggled to resurrect them, but spare parts were often unavailable.

'Reliable on All Fronts...'
Such dramatic advertisements frequently appeared in the various German newspapers and periodicals.

Maximum Capacity
A heavy-duty Zündapp K 800 sidecar combination seems to be overloaded with crewmembers, members of the Luftwaffe ground forces. All carry Mauser carbines and MP38/40 submachine guns. The well-worn front tire speaks of miles of service while the horseshoe indicates membership of a cavalry detachment.

Well-Suited

In a photo taken in 1941, motorcycle troops wear both First World War-era Model 18 *stahlhelm* (with lug nuts or 'horn rivets' for attaching a protective metal faceplate) and later new-style M40 steel helmets as well as their *kradmantel* overcoats.

Opposite below: Hanover Zündapp

A German army officer has apparently managed to keep his Zündapp K 500 out of uniform. The IS registration plate indicates its home in the Hanover area of Lower Saxony.

The city's name was employed in two major actions of the war. The first, Operation Hanover, took place near Smolensk at Vyazma during April–June 1942 and involved the German elimination of Soviet airborne troops and partisans seeking to disrupt the rear sectors of the German Army Group Centre and the 4th Army in particular. With over 10,000 Red Army casualties and 20,000 prisoners taken, the operation qualified officially as the most successful of the many anti-partisan campaigns and prevented partisan activity from reforming for the remainder of the war. Operation Hanover II came within the same time period and took place near Moscow with the destruction of the Soviet 39th Army and 22nd Cavalry Corps.

Hanover also played a significant role in the Nazi anti-Jewish action known as Kristalnacht of 9 November 1938, resulting in the destruction of Jewish synagogues and businesses across Germany. Because his family was deported to Poland, Herschel Grynszpan, then living in Paris, shot and killed a German diplomat. The Nazis used this as an excuse to conduct the nation-wide pogrom. During the years of the Third Reich seven concentration camps were also established in Hanover, with slave labour being used in the local factories. Few of the city's 4,800 Jewish residents survived the war.

Hanover, also an important railway and production centre, became a strategic target, resulting in eighty-eight Allied bombing attacks; only 10 per cent of its original structures survived the war and some 6,000 civilians were killed.

Fallschirmjäger and NSU Kettenkrad

An elite airborne trooper employs an HK 101 for a souvenir photo. Rather than a motorcycle per se, the Kettenkrad was a 'small half-track prime mover' designed to carry cargo or tow small artillery pieces, functioning as a multi-purpose all-terrain workhorse. Patented in 1939 and put into production by NSU, it was powered by a 36 hp, four-cylinder Opel Olympia auto engine. It could reach speeds of 70 km/h and climb a 60 per cent grade. Some 10,000 were produced during the war, with production continuing briefly post-war when the versatile Kettenkrad's duties transferred to employment in agriculture.

The Fallschirmjäger proved their value early in the war in strategic German assaults but after taking part in the semi-abortive airborne attack on the British-held island of Crete, during which they incurred very high casualties, Hitler effectively grounded them. They later proved their reputation again in Italy when Allied forces tried to dislodge them from the famous Monte Cassino battleground.

Kettenkrad – 10 December 1942 – *Berlin Illustrated News*
Albert Speer, the Third Reich's chief architect and Armaments Minister, seemingly enjoys piloting the newest model of the Kettenkrad, which was designed to overcome the sea of mud as encountered on the Eastern Front. At this pivotal date in the war Stalingrad was a massive blood bath, consuming some 2 million German and Russian troops. Ground troops sent to relieve the encircled 6th Army and portions of the 4th Army as well as Luftwaffe efforts to drop supplies from the air failed, and the surviving 100,000 Axis troops surrendering into Soviet captivity on 23 January 1943 – the point at which the tide of the war changed from German offense to defence. Fewer than 5,000 of the German POWs would ever return home.

Celebratory Stamp
A postage stamp, one of a series celebrating the German military, features the unusual Kettenkrad tracked vehicle cresting a hill. The stamp's price of 4 pfennigs includes an additional 3 pfennig 'war tax'.

'Tank Buster'
This BMW R12 carries a Steib sidecar modified to carry anti-tank armaments as this soldier had the dubious task of taking on Russian tanks. The so-called 'tank buster' is fitted with dual-purpose on and off-road treaded front tire and 'blacked out' headlamp providing only a sliver of light in the darkness.

The Army corporal wears the Iron Cross Second Class (EK II), indicating he has already seen combat. The civilian license plate indicates the motorcycle was originally registered in Stuttgart while insignia appearing on the sidecar identify it as belonging to Panzer Jaeger Division 652. The *jaeger* ('hunter') designation indicates a 'light' (*leichte*) division reduced in size to only two regiments and trained to fight on difficult terrain. Notations on the reverse of the photo establish the location as St Dinan in north-western France, a medieval walled Breton town overlooking the river Rance. The photograph is also dated as 24 June 1940 and was taken to mark the awarding of the soldier's medal for bravery. Further handwritten notes include personal words addressed to *Liebe Mutti* (the soldier's mother) with vestiges of glue indicating the photo was once held within an album.

The French had surrendered to German forces three days previously on 21 June, the armistice being signed, under Hitler's direction, at Compiègne in the same railway car in which the Germans had surrendered in November 1918 at the end of the First World War. On 25 June, a day after the photo was taken, the official ceasefire went into effect in France with the toll of casualties eventually tabulated as 85,000 French, 3,475 British and 27,074 German.

Stamp of Approval
E. Meerwald, a leading graphic designer well known for his dramatic film posters, designed this stamp, though it is inaccurate in detail. By its printing date of 1943, motorcycle troop units had been officially disbanded. In addition, the BMW R11 depicted is an obsolete model that appeared in 1929 and was out of production by 1935, having been replaced by the R12.

Bolt of Lightning
Stretching into the distance along a French village roadway, a line of motorcycle riflemen lead an assault aboard 750cc BMW R12 sidecar combinations. Insignia including the crooked arrow indicate a communications/scouting tasked group. Note that the headlamp black-out covers have been removed during daytime hours.

Unser Heer
Schnelle Truppen: Kradschützen im Gefecht

'Our Army – Fast Assault Troops – Motorcycle Infantry in Battle'

The image of a gas-masked German soldier having disembarked from a *kradschützen* sidecar promotes the image of the mobile infantry and its application of the motorcycle. The illustration appeared in a series of state-produced postcards highlighting various elements of the *Heer* in action.

Four Comrades

A photo from a soldier's album bears an inscription in vermillion ink, penned long after the photograph was taken. The massive engine cases and exhaust pipe helps identify the motorcycle as a 1930s Victoria Bergmeister; the 596cc OHV four-stroke, twin-cylinder producing 18 hp, with some 67,000 having been produced before the war between 1932 and 1938.

Mobile Barber's Chair
A Luftwaffe flak NCO gets a haircut aboard a BMW 'flying chair'.

Lederhosen
Troopers in the popular Bavarian-style leather breeches, considered a sign of virility and strength, pose alongside their standard army uniformed comrades with a 750cc BMW R12 driven sidecar in centre position.

SS Jawa Prototype

With the occupation of Czechoslovakia in 1938, Germany's war effort gained access to its considerable weapons manufacturing facilities, including the world-renowned Skoda Armaments Works. Other Czech companies that fell under the Third Reich's shadow included the motorcycles produced by Jawa ('Ya-wa'). Seen here is a rare factory photo of a prototype single-cylinder machine bearing the SS runes.

Jawa motorcycles was founded in 1929 by Frantisek Janecek, a mechanical designer previously known for developing a successful hand grenade. He devised the company's name from the first two letters of his name and his first motorcycle, the Austrian Wanderer. While he started with a 500cc machine, he moved on to small displacement 175cc two-strokes that, because of price and design, became very successful. German occupation in 1938 caused a switch to building airplane engines, but development began on an advanced 250cc single-cylinder two-stroke with rounded lines – most likely the prototype seen here and photographed with the SS registration plate (perhaps to camouflage their efforts inasmuch as the Jawa employers and employees both actively sabotaged their German war production). The new Jawa never fell into the hands of the SS and eventually went into post-war production for the civilian market.

SS Man and Girlfriend

The civilian machine appears to be a DKW RT125 and still wears its Pomeranian area registration plates and a black-out-equipped headlamp.

Double Lightning Bolt Insignia
SS motorcycle troops stand at the ready by their
BMW R12 (left) and DKW NZ350 (right) machines,
their fender-mounted license plates marked with the
dreaded twin lightning bolts. The SS were Hitler's
'ideological soldiers', charged with hunting down all
perceived enemies of Nazi Germany. Waffen-SS units
were more battlefield directed but some also took
active roles in the 'ethnic cleansing' that consumed
millions of lives.

Reaping the Whirlwind
A *kradschützen* pauses between two DKWs to watch the progress of Waffen SS
Totenkopfverbände troops marching through a Russian grain field.

The original Totenkopfverbande or Death's Head division were SS members trained as
concentration camp personnel under the direction of the fanatical Theodore Eicke. By order of
Hitler and Himmler, Eicke had executed SA leader Ernst Roehm in his prison cell after Roehm
refused the offer of suicide.

Eicke strove to develop a combat arm of the Totenkopfverbande (SSTK) and through his
brutal emphasis on rigorous training, racist indoctrination and iron discipline as well as intense
esprit de corps, he created one of the most successful and notorious Waffen-SS divisions. Its
members saw continuous combat for nearly four years on the Eastern Front, often being called
in as a 'fire brigade' at critical battlefield junctures to meet the ever-increasing and eventually
unstoppable power of the Red Army. On 26 February 1943 Eicke died after his light aircraft, a
Fieseler Storch, was shot down by Russian ground fire when he went to investigate the status of
one of his SS units at the village of Michailovka.

Brief Summer of Victory
Waffen-SS Totenkopfverbande troops enjoy their first Russian summer along with a meal. A Zündapp DB200 is visible in the background wearing SS plates.

Known for their bravado in battle, the SSTK suffered high casualties as the war ground closer to Germany's borders. Their fanaticism slowed the Soviet advance but eventually resulted in the near annihilation of their formations, which devolved through regroupings into both tank and infantry forces as well as motorcycle troops. In May 1945 surviving members made an effort to surrender to the Americans but were turned over to the Soviets, where they received the treatment the Russians reserved for members of the SS. Guilty of the murder of French and Russian civilians and British POWs, the Waffen-SS including the SSTK were adjudged criminal organisations in post-war war crimes investigations, the Totenkopfverbande also having been intrinsically linked with the slave labour and extermination camps.

'Motorcycle Messenger on the Eastern Front' – 26 May 1942
The cover of *Germany Illustrated* spotlights motorcycle troops and a well-worn, relatively rare R66 sport model BMW enduring the rigors of the Eastern Front. The registration plate has been blotted out by military censors. Now entering the second year of the invasion of Soviet Union, General von Manstein's forces had begun the long siege of Sevastopol in early May. On the very day of the news magazine's publication, 26 May, Rommel's Afrika Korps were clanking across the North African desert toward Tobruk, driving the British out of Libya. However on the next day, back in Europe, British-trained Czech commandos assassinated the ruthless SS leader Reinhard Heydrich, leading to bloody reprisals against the Czech people.

Crossroads for a Motorcycle Courier in Russia
Stepping off his DKW NZ350, a soldier stops for a photograph establishing his presence on
the Eastern Front. The cluster of handmade signage directs toward various unit staging areas,
supply centres and field hospitals.

Preparing for Transport
What appears to be an NSU is winched aboard a transport ship bound for one of the distant
shores on which the Germany army travelled. Hundreds of Wehrmacht motorcycles now lie
rusting beneath the sea, their supply ships having been sunk by Allied submarine or aircraft.

River Crossing
Combat engineers (Pioneers) paddle an inflatable raft carrying two BMW sidecar rigs. While explosions can be seen in the distance, the white denim fatigues, the condition of the motorcycles and the relatively relaxed appearance of the soldiers indicate a training exercise in progress.

The various engineer units, known collectively as *Pioniere*, included *Pioniertruppen* (Pioneer Troops), *Bautruppen* (Construction Troops), *Eisenbahntruppen* (Railway Troops), and *Technische Truppen* (Technical Troops). While assigned different construction work goals, all were first and foremost assault troops as well as skilled in explosive demolition and mine detection.

Ripples of the Russian Invasion
Both solo and sidecar machines traverse a river, following in the progress of a personnel carrier. Russian civilians observing the action can be glimpsed to the left and in the background. German forces encountered untold numbers of rivers, lakes, streams, bogs and swamps as they moved through the vastness of the Soviet Union – a vastness that would swallow them up.

Hot Coffee/Cold Motorcycle

Dealing with an unexpected military diversion, Hitler was forced to come to the aid of his Italian allies floundering in the Balkans. It led to a delay in the planned invasion of the Soviet Union, an upset to the timetable and German forces battling Russia's formidable ally, General Winter, and leading to its ultimate failure to quickly conquer the Soviet Union, which Hitler and his generals were certain would 'fall like a house of cards' in a matter of weeks – and summer weeks at that.

Never Warm Enough

Kradschützen found insufficient warmth even with their vaunted *kradmantel* overcoats.

Confronting their first Eastern Front winter, and equipped with only their relatively lightweight summer uniforms, thousands of German soldiers and their weapons succumbed to the blizzard conditions. Motorcyclists, along with their foot soldier *kameraden*, resorted to eating the horse meat provided by the 100,000 horses and mules that died in the freezing cold. But the iron horses, like this Zündapp, soldiered on.

Misery at -30 F
A DKW NZ350 (right) and a lightweight DKW RT125 (left) have been piled high with gear and blankets. The three soldiers, their helmets white-washed in an attempt to camouflage them from snipers, manage to pose for a photo in the Russian winter landscape.

Spring Thaw – Russian Front
The German word for mud is *schlamm*, which somehow captures both the feel and sound of it, at least for the soldiers struggling with their heavyweight Zündapp KS 600.

The other side of the double-bladed Russian climate was the rainy season or *rasputitsa* when the snow melted, turning the roads into quagmires – muddy oceans that sapped the strength of man and machine trapped in its suffocating grip. By autumn the roads had turned into nearly impassable bogs; the fields over which the motorcycles travelled turning into 'seas of jelly'. The same thing would happen again of course in the following spring. The Soviets had a phrase for it – 'time without roads'.

Traversing the Russian 'Corduroy Road'
Weary and dust-covered Waffen-SS troops watch a NSU mounted dispatch rider negotiate a hastily constructed log road designed to bridge ravines and provide a solid foundation over the enervating mud. Such widespread means to battle the muddy conditions with wooden logs resulted in the term 'corduroy road'.

A significant side effect of the mud was the drain on fuel supplies, particularly for heavy motorized vehicles, including the all-important panzers. Where a certain number of gallons would enable a vehicle to travel hundreds of kilometres, the quagmire reduced the distances to a few hundred meters.

End of the Russian Line
Apparently without help, a soldier attempts to load his BMW sidecar onto a train car standing at the end of the rail line. Fortunately it wasn't the 880-lb R75 but the lighter 500 sidevalve model. It's likely the engine was running and his hand was on the throttle as he edged it up the ramp.

The Wehrmacht was hampered in its supply efforts in part due to the smaller gauge of the Soviet rail lines, requiring time-consuming reconstruction; indications of the rebuilding materials are visible in the photograph's background.

Italians Far from Home
In cooperation with his German allies and in quest of a piece of the Russian pie, Mussolini ordered some 250,000 troops to fight on the Eastern Front – a far cry from their warm Mediterranean climate. They brought with them a variety of Italian motorcycles, principally the Moto Guzzi Alce 500cc single-cylinder solo mount. An Italian Breda machine gun was often mounted to the handlebars and such motorized troops were employed as fast assault units.

Seen here are a group of Bersaglieri, elite troops who wore distinctive feather-plumed headgear and built a reputation for courage under fire that even the often disdainful Germans acknowledged. Eventually, tens of thousands of Italian troops would fall on the Russian Front; thousands more were killed or suffered as slave labourers under the Germans themselves after Italy switched allegiance to the Allies near the end of the war.

Bulgarian Temporary Allies
A German sidevalve BMW's 'B' designation plate identifies it as a Bulgarian-commissioned machine. Initially neutral under King Boris, the constitutional monarchy's government eventually gravitated toward the Axis to prevent a German invasion and to regain territory lost in the First World War. While Bulgarian forces did occupy parts of Yugoslavia and Greece under the German flag, the king and his people resisted, allowing the Nazi extermination of its Jewish citizens. King Boris died suddenly, apparently having been poisoned, and the country was then torn by between Axis and anti-Axis forces. As the war's tide turned against Germany, pro-communist Bulgarian elements took control, with its armed forces joining Soviet troops in the last stages of the war.

Spanish Volunteers – Division Azul

Depictions of German-uniformed Spanish troops wrestling a Zündapp through the Russian winter appeared on food ration stamps issued by the Fascist Franco regime. Spain, having recently fought its own bloody civil war with the aid of Nazi Germany, chose neutrality during the Second World War. However, Franco, a fervent anti-communist, allowed Spanish citizens to fight in Soviet Russia, but not against the Western Allies. The Azul, or 'Blue Division', 250th Infantry Division eventually totalled some 45,000 volunteers seeing action from June 1941 at the very outset of the invasion of the Soviet Union. The Germans considered their Spanish allies highly undisciplined, but equals in combat. Joining the German 16th Army, the Division Azul fought both at Stalingrad and during the Siege of Leningrad. While Franco recalled them in late 1943, many chose to fight on to the very last days of the Battle of Berlin. In all, 5,000 were KIA and 8,700 were wounded, with Spanish POWs remaining in captivity until April 1954.

Cycle Protestors – 27 March 1941 – Belgrade, Yugoslavia
Under extreme duress, the Yugoslavian government succumbed to Nazi Germany's ultimatum to join the Axis Tripartite Agreement; the documents were signed on 25 March 1941. Two days later, the Serbian people and elements of the army took to the streets, chanting, 'Rather war than the pact, rather death than slavery.' The government was overthrown, the Serbs taking an anti-Nazi stance. In response to the Serbian defiance, Hitler ordered the destruction of Yugoslavia as a military power and sovereign state. Belgrade was subsequently bombed on 6 April, resulting in more than 17,000 deaths. Four days later German forces and their Italian and Bulgarian allies attacked the country, overpowering Yugoslav forces within two weeks. The Germans then carved up the country, creating an independent Croatian state – its fascist Ustase turning on its Serbian and Jewish fellow citizens, murdering hundreds of thousands.

Rare American Appearance

A young Serbian soldier is photographed with a Harley-Davidson VL. The model first appeared in 1936, with this one somehow making its way to Yugoslavia. The 80-cubic-inch motor could reach 90 mph. Note the foot clutch and tank-mounted gear shifter.

The young soldier's fate is unknown. The Nazi-supported fascist Ustase regime in Croatia, in power during 1941–45, launched a genocidal war against the Serbs, their long-time fellow countrymen having shared what had been Yugoslavia. At least 300,000 Serbs were murdered, 250,000 were expelled and 200,000 were forcibly converted to Catholicism. The barbarity of the Croatians even appalled their Nazi allies. In one 'throat cutting contest' a single Croatian guard murdered over 1,300 prisoners.

Imbalance

Attempting to defy gravity, and a steep hillside, a BMW R12 has landed upside down in a ravine.

End Result
Another view of the sidecar reveals its previous occupants – a pair of motorcycle troopers, apparently uninjured, except perhaps for their pride. The corporal and NCO await help, with rescuers and their horses visible on the horizon.

Mobile Medic
Medical units also relied on motorcycle transport. Here a *sanitätssoldat* tends to a wounded soldier amid the mangled wreckage of what may be a sidecar or small troop-carrying cart, which may have taken enemy fire or tumbled down the hillside.

Burning Motorcycle
While it bears Wehrmacht registration plates, the insignia on the exhaust indicates it may have been a requisitioned French machine.

War's End in North Africa – Self-Propelled POWs
Against a backdrop of thousands of once-vaunted Afrika Korps troops, a crowded Zündapp pulling a small trailer brings more German prisoners to an Allied assembly area in Tunisia.

Civilian DKW and Wounded Hitler Youth Soldier – May 1945
The image appeared among a series of collector cards, Series 58 'The Second World War in Pictures,' as produced in post-war West Germany.

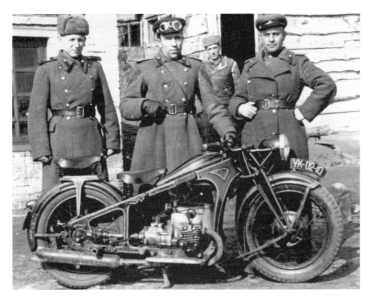

New Owners
Red Army soldiers pose with a German Zündapp, now displaying Soviet registration.

'Unfortunate Accident'
While serving in a Luftwaffe communications (*Luftnachtrichten*) detachment in western France, twenty-three-year-old Corporal Franz Berger, a blacksmith's son from Engersdorf, Austria, died on 29 May 1943 from injuries sustained while riding a motorcycle. On the night of the same day, back in Germany, 90 per cent of Barmen-Wuppertal was destroyed by a RAF bombing raid – one of thousands of such aerial assaults that would churn most of Germany's cities into rubble.

Ein Held ist, wer sein Leben Großem opfert.

KIA Motorcyclist and Multiple Graves

Found on the reverse of the photo, biographical information describes Lt Ludwig Schlander as the company commander of a motorcycle troop who took part in the Western, Polish and Eastern campaigns, during which he was awarded both the 2nd and 1st Class Iron Cross, the Infantry Combat badge, the Wound Badge in Silver and the East Medal. He was killed in action on 25 February 1943 in Russia, his 'hero's grave' being located in the vicinity of Kirejkowo near Bolechow. A further inscription on his memorial card reads: *Ein Held is, wer sein Leben Grossem opfert* – 'A Hero is one who sacrifices his Life.'

The location of Schlander's gravesite, the Ukrainian town of Bolchow, aka Bolechow, was first occupied by German allied battalions of the Hungarian-Slovakian army on 6 July 1941 after the retreat of Red Army forces following the massive German invasion of the USSR on 21 June.

After rounding up the town's Jewish residents, numbering over 5,000, they were first stripped of their valuables then forced into hard labour as the local Ukrainian militia continued to rob and abuse them. It was followed by the first *aktion* that took place on 28 October 1941, when a number of Jewish men and women were driven into a building, its chimney blocked to produce fumes from a burning fire. The women were stripped and forced to dance while the men were beaten. Members of the German police and the Ukrainian militia then forced them into the nearby Tenyava forest where a mass grave had been dug. Because of the shortage of bullets, the wounded were buried alive. A second *aktion* followed on 20 August 1942 that involved sixty hours of torture upon a large group of Jews assembled by Germans and their Ukrainian volunteers. Those that survived, of which there were approximately 4,000, were packed in cattle cars and sent to their deaths at the Belzec death camp. Bolechow was just one of thousands of such towns and villages across Eastern Europe decimated by the Germans and their collaborators.

Deathcard for a Dispatch Rider

Army *Gefreiter Kradmelder* (Lance Corporal motorcyclist) Michael Scherr, a farmer's son from Hiltenbach, following one and a half years of service and previously awarded the Wound Badge, returned for his second posting on the Eastern Front. He was killed there on 18 June 1944 at the age of twenty and was buried at Mohileff near Minsk.

Soviet troops, when encountering German battlefield cemeteries, and the number grew rapidly as the war ground on, often used tanks to obliterate all traces of the hated enemy. Currently extensive efforts are in progress to locate and disinter German war dead and either return them to Germany or rebury them in newly established memorial sites across Eastern Europe.

Two of Millions

Somewhere in a sun-soaked field lie the graves of corporals Konrad Bugenstock and Willi Dahm, who died together on 18 May 1940. The date indicates the time when Guderian's panzers were blitzkrieging across Belgium on their way to France where German forces, during early May, attacked the vaunted Maginot defensive line from the rear, enabling the encirclement of French army resulting in the imminent fall of France, with years of carnage to follow.

The photograph, taken by a comrade in arms, identifies the KIA as members of a motorcycle rifle troop, as indicated by the registration plate left on the grave along with the carefully placed wildflowers. The license plate was once attached to the front fender of their motorcycle and the non-military 'IT' designation indicates the machine originated in the district of Hessen-Nassau, apparently having been conscripted from civilian life, as were its riders.

Blick von den Höhen.(17)

The Descent
A page from a soldier's service album includes a neatly typed caption that reads 'View from the Heights'. The photograph was taken prior to the precipitous fall of the so-called Thousand Year Reich that lasted but twelve.

Fading Memories
The American General Douglas McArthur once observed, 'Old soldiers just fade away.' The silhouetted image of three *kradmelder* still evokes distinct memories for the veterans of the Second World War, as do all such photos. As of 2017, the veterans of all the war's combatant countries were themselves fading away at the rate of a thousand per day.

Memories Revised – 'Vikings Under Fire'

Der Landser magazine's cover illustration refers to the 1941 Eastern Front and the motorcycle troops of the Waffen-SS Viking Division. The story itself was titled 'Vikings Under Fire', 'Where Death is their Companion'. The issue focused on the battle at Pulkovo in the summer of 1943 and the Soviet breakthrough on the Eastern Front as reported by an 'eye-witness' Luftwaffe pilot.

The elite troops of the Viking Division consisted of volunteers from Holland, Belgium, Denmark and Norway under German command, formed from three motorized infantry regiments joined by an attached Finnish volunteer infantry battalion, the Finns having previously fought the Soviets during the Winter War of 1940. The Viking Division also contained artillery, anti-aircraft, combat engineer, reconnaissance, tank and anti-tank battalions. While they did engage Soviet troops, some also took part in *aktions* against Jews as well as other 'enemies of Germany'. The infamous 'Angel of Death' Josef Mengele was a Viking Division member. Eventually decimated during 1944, remnants of the group fought in Hungary against the Soviets, with the survivors eventually surrendering in May 1945.

Characterised as a 'pulp magazine', *Der Landser* first appeared in 1957 – the series claiming to feature 'authentic stories of the Second World War' with much of its content focused on the campaign against the Russians. Its title refers to the name given to the common soldier and while claiming to stand for peace, its content consistently glorified war and painted a distorted image of Nazi Germany, omitting any mention of its crimes or its repressive dictatorship. Summing up the publication's agenda, Germany's leading news publication *Der Spiegel* had called it 'the expert journal for the whitewashing of the Wehrmacht'. *Der Landser* was available to readers throughout Germany, Austria, Belgium, Switzerland, Luxembourg, France and Italy.

In September 2013, the German publisher Bauer Media, after many challenges over the years to its subject matter, announced it would stop publishing *Der Landser* after it was criticized by an American Jewish group for heroic portrayals of German war criminals in the Second World War, although the publishers protested that the magazine simply offered tales of ordinary soldiers in the war. However, the Los Angeles Simon Wiesenthal Center brought forth documentation demonstrating how officers and units portrayed by the magazine were involved in the mass murder of Jews or partisans and other atrocities.

Non-innocent Bystanders
A motorcycle trooper prepares his camera to record the hanging of three men executed for violating one of the many Nazi civil, military, political and racial 'crimes' that were punishable by death.

   Postscript: One must not forget that the motorcycle soldiers of the Third Reich were part and parcel of a criminal regime responsible for a war of aggression resulting in the deaths of 50 million men, women and children.